The Jack Ruby Trial Revisited

The Diary of Jury Foreman Max Causey

The
Jack Ruby Trial
Revisited

THE DIARY OF
JURY FOREMAN MAX CAUSEY

Edited by John Mark Dempsey

University of North Texas Press • Denton, Texas

Printed in the United States of America.
First edition 2000
10 9 8 7 6 5 4 3 2 1

Permissions:
University of North Texas Press
PO Box 311336
Denton TX 76203-1336

The paper used in this book meets the minimum requirements of the American
National Standard for Permanence of Paper for Printed Library Materials,
z39.48.1984. Binding materials have been chosen for durability.

Library of Congress Cataloging-in-Publication Data

Causey, Max, 1928–1997.
The Jack Ruby trial revisited: the diary of jury foreman Max Causey/
Edited by J.M. Dempsey.
p.   cm.
Includes bibliographical references and index.
ISBN 1-57441-121-7 (alk. Paper)
1.Ruby, Jack—Trials, litigation, etc. 2. Trials (Murder)—Texas—Dallas
3. Causey, Max, 1928-1997—Diaries.
4. Jury—Texas—Dallas—Biography.
I. Dempsey, J.M. (John Mark), 1954– II. Title.
KF224.R8 C38 2000
345.73'02523—dc21
00-009042

Design by Angela Schmitt

To Max Causey's family: Rosemary, Keith, Kevin, and Gina

Acknowledgments

With thanks to the staff members of the UNT Press for their invaluable assistance on this project. Also, thanks to Gary Mack of the Sixth Floor Museum in Dallas for his help.

Contents

Jurors from left to right: Luther E. Dickerson, Mildred McCollum, Max Causey, Aileen B. Shields, Robert J. Flechtner, Gwen English, J. G. Holton, Jr., Douglas Sowell, James E. Cunningham, J. Waymon Rose, Louise Malone, and Allen W. McCoy

Introduction

"The Carl Sandburgs of the future
will spend whole lifetimes trying to
analyze the drama of this week and
this scene. What it all comes down to—
after the assassination of a president,
the wounding of a governor, the slaying
of a policeman, and the killing of a
man nobody really knew—is little
Jack Ruby."
—Syndicated columnist Dorothy
Kilgallen, February 1964

The men and women who served as the jurors in the trial of Jack Ruby were both exceptional and ordinary. Exceptional in that it became their singular duty to sit in judgment of a man who played a bizarre and bloody role in perhaps the most controversial event of the twentieth century. Ordinary in that nothing in their lives before or after the trial in February and March of 1964 has distinguished them from millions of their fellow citizens. Like most of us, they lived happily in quiet anonymity with the glaring exception of the nearly four weeks of the Ruby trial. For those few weeks, their pictures, names, and life stories appeared countless times in newspapers and magazines worldwide. Yet, within a few days after the trial, they gladly melted back into obscurity. In talking with surviving jurors for this book, it is remarkable what little lasting effect the trial had on their lives, although one (Bob Flechtner) says the trial at least indirectly caused him to leave a new job he had just begun when the court proceedings began.

They would be bitterly criticized for their decision no matter what it was. If they found Ruby not guilty, they would be considered examples of Dallas' alleged frontier-justice mentality, which, so much of the country believed, caused the death of John F. Kennedy, and then, his accused assassin, Lee Harvey Oswald. If they found him guilty of first-degree murder, and sentenced him to death, they would be accused of trying to atone for Dallas' sins by sacrificing the life of the brawling strip joint owner. If they found him guilty and sentenced him to some lesser punishment, no one with strong feelings about the case would be satisfied. The country, cheated of a trial of the hapless Oswald, would instead focus its attention on the proceedings against Ruby.

The first juror selected, and the eventual foreman of the jury, was Max Causey. During the course of the trial, Causey kept a handwritten diary in a stenographer's notebook. He considered writing a book about his memories of the trial, and did write a short memoir, "The Trial of a Juror," within a year or two of the trial's end. Shortly after he died suddenly in September 1997, his family gave permission to J. M. Dempsey, Causey's nephew, to develop a book based on his diary, memoir, and the many personal letters that the Causeys received during the trial, many of which also appear in this book.

At the time of the Ruby trial, Max Causey was a thirty-five-year-old administrative engineer in charge of cost analysis, scheduling, and forecasting with the defense contractor Ling-Temco-Vought, which became E-Systems and eventually Raytheon. He retired in 1990. His supervisor at LTV called him "likable, easy to get along with, and cheerful." He grew up in the country east of Dallas, near the small town of Caddo Mills. He earned a bachelor's degree in government from East Texas State College (now Texas A&M University-Commerce) in 1950, and a master's degree in education from East Texas State in 1962. Causey received a commission in the U.S. Air Force in 1950, received pilot training, and flew a refueling tanker at Vance Air Force Base in Enid, Oklahoma, and Davis-Monthan Air Force Base in Tucson, Arizona. He left the Air Force in 1955 as a first lieutenant. He married Rosemary Middlebrooks of Commerce in 1953, and they had two sons, Keith, who was born in 1955, and Kevin, who was born in 1957 and died of natural causes in 1966. They adopted a daughter, Gina, in 1967. Max was a longtime leader in the First Baptist Church of Garland, serving for a time as chairman of deacons ("Juror praised" 1964; K. Causey, et al., 2000).

Causey comments in his diary that he started writing his "daily log of activities" on the second day of his term as a juror, so it appears the first day's notes were written from very fresh memory. He continued keeping notes day-by-day as the trial continued, ending on Saturday, March 14, when the jury delivered its verdict. He then wrote a short epilogue, apparently very soon after the trial concluded. Sometime later, Causey wrote a memoir from the diary he kept during the trial. Both the memoir and the diary are presented in this book, augmented with editor's notes taken from the trial transcripts, books, and newspaper and magazine articles.

What comes across in the diary is a young man very concerned about meeting his responsibilities to his family and his employer, but, between the lines, in a way that would seem foreign to many of us today, proud and excited to serve:

> Many times during these many days have I asked my-
> self "Why me, why did I allow myself to be accepted
> for this jury?" Several times during my qualification
> questioning I could have answered either the state or
> the defense in such a manner as to have had the court
> disqualify me as a juror. Why, then, did I not do this?
> The answer is simple. I could not do so without sacri-
> ficing those legal and moral aspects of our society that
> I hold most reverent.

The Ruby trial is inextricably linked with the assassination of President Kennedy and the many conspiracy theories surrounding the roles of both Lee Harvey Oswald and Jack Ruby, and Causey maintained a lifelong interest in the lore surrounding the assassination. "From the very beginning, I think he was a staunch believer that there was nothing to it [an assassination conspiracy]," his son Keith says. "As the years went by, I think he became a little more questioning, or accepting of the possibility that there might have been something more [involved in the assassination] than Lee Oswald.

"He never, ever, ever wavered from his belief that Ruby acted totally alone. That was never a question, because he always said that Ruby was not stable enough for the Mafia or the CIA to put any stock in at all. He felt like Ruby was something of a 'wild card' and that's not your typical kind of Mafia hit man."

Causey also had no second thoughts about the jury's verdict and the death sentence rendered. "He had no regrets about the verdict at all," his widow, Rosemary Causey, says. But Keith says he doesn't believe his father was distressed when the Texas Court of Criminal Appeals overturned the case in 1966, although the younger Causey does not remember the decision. "I think he felt like Ruby deserved the death penalty, but I don't know that he necessarily wanted to see him executed," Keith says. "He felt like he did what was justified and right, but I don't think he necessarily wanted to see him go to the electric chair as a result of what he did."

During jury deliberations, Causey initially voted for a life sentence for Ruby, explaining in his memoir that he wanted to be sure the jury had a chance to fully discuss the question of Ruby's sentence. "I can remember when I first found out that there was somebody who had voted not to give him [Ruby] the death penalty, I thought it was probably one of the women. But when I found out it was him, wow, it was something of a surprise," Keith says.

Mrs. Causey says Max had a clear idea of why Ruby shot Oswald. "He really thought that Ruby thought he was going to be a hero, because he was going to kill the guy who shot the president."

Causey's family believes the idea is preposterous that he or any jury members were motivated by a desire to vindicate the city of Dallas. "That's nonsense. I don't think he ever felt Dallas was to blame for what happened anyway," Keith says. "To me that was an excuse made up by defense lawyers or the media. I know for a fact that never entered his mind, and I can't really imagine that it ever entered any of those people's minds. Only a very small percentage of people ever blamed the city of Dallas for what happened anyway."

To the people who knew him, it was not surprising that Max Causey became the leader of the Ruby jury, although he would not have sought the role. "He wasn't overtly that way [a leader]. He had a calm, self-assured way he went about doing things," Keith says.

Mrs. Causey says her husband was "a super guy . . . Max would do anything for anybody. He was outreach leader [the person who makes contact with members who are sick or having some sort of trouble] in Sunday school for years. And I kept saying, 'Why don't you let them vote for somebody else?' And he said, 'Well, they always just say, "You take it."' He took it and he worked like a dog on it." Causey arranged for church members to sit up around the clock for a member who died just five months before he himself died. "They'd be willing to go sit in the hospital if Dad said to do it," recalls Gina (Causey) Rothwell, Max's daughter.

"He was one of these kind of people: You tend to do it [a task] because you know you're going to do it the way you want it done," Keith observes.

Mrs. Causey remembers her husband as a sober, responsible man, always prepared for the worst eventuality. "Max was a very dependable guy. But he was a pessimist from the word go," she says. "I was the proverbial optimist, and everybody laughed about him being a pessimist. When he was going through pilot's school, he was always going to fail. Always, always, always. Of course, he always did super great. He was always better than he thought he was."

"I think part of his pessimism was to tone down some of her optimism," Keith wryly observes. "You have to go overboard one way to bring it all back to level. He was always trying to prepare everyone for the worst, and if the best comes along, that's fine and good. But be prepared if it doesn't work out that way. You can tell by the way he left his affairs in order. He prepared everything very well."

More so than the other jurors, Causey was caught in the harsh glare of publicity surrounding the trial. "I remember the day that they gave the sentence, death, on television, my phone rang immediately. She [the caller] said, 'That husband of yours needs to be shot right through the head.' I will never forget that. I cried like everything," Mrs. Causey remembers. "I didn't realize till it was over with, our house was patrolled [by police] every night, because they were afraid somebody would do something to the house."

Although admittedly just eight years old at the time of the Ruby trial, Keith says the family had no fears related to the many conspiracy theories that have grown up over the years surrounding the deaths of people connected in some way to the JFK assassination. "That had never even been suggested," he says. "Knowing what I know now, and had you thrust me back to March of '64, I might have started thinking about all the conspiracy things."

After Max arrived home in a sheriff's car after the trial, the family escaped to his parents' home near Caddo Mills to avoid the harassing phone calls and media onslaught. "We had to leave immediately. It was on TV, us pulling out of our driveway," Mrs. Causey remembers. "The guy was interviewing him as he walked up the sidewalk. He got in the car and [the reporter] asked a question through the window, and we backed out and drove off."

Mrs. Causey remembers the horde of reporters that descended on their suburban Garland home when her husband was selected as a juror. "What shocked me was, the day he was chosen as a juror, I had nine reporters in my living room wanting to know all about Max. 'What did he request [to be brought to him at the courthouse]?' I remember he wanted his red jumpsuit," Mrs. Causey says with a laugh. "[They] wanted to know what Max thought about Kevin [the Causey's child who was afflicted with a mentally debilitating disease]. In the paper, it said, 'Max calls him our angel.'" Kevin died from the disease two years later.

For some of the surviving jurors who were interviewed for this book, the Ruby trial was only a footnote in their lives, a distant, seldom-recalled memory. To Causey, the trial had a much greater impact. "None of the others got nearly the publicity that Dad did," Keith recalls. "The second, fifth and eighth jurors chosen, they didn't have [CBS News reporter] Nelson Benton knocking on their door, didn't have [WFAA-TV reporter] Murphy Martin. It was unique because he was the first. It was an event for Dad. Not only was he the first one, he was the foreman. He signed the verdict. There was so much of it that was his. To a lot of the other people, it may have just been another trial. I don't know if [juror Allen] McCoy's kids thought of it the way I did. I just got all interested in this stuff, and so, all the Kennedy stuff therefore interested me, and I've read all those books [related to the JFK assassination]."

Upon his death in September 1997, Causey's name once again hit the newspapers and the airwaves. "I was floored. I could not believe that," Mrs. Causey says of the obituaries and broadcast news items. "It was everywhere. A lot of our friends called. We got a letter from one of them, way out somewhere. I think [a friend's] son saw it in Oklahoma. I would have thought he would have been long forgotten."

Gina, the Causeys' daughter, was not born at the time of the Ruby trial. "It never was important to me," she remembers. "Dad would tell me he was on it, and Mom would say this was a big deal. But I didn't know what it was.

"When I was in high school I had a history teacher. We were talking about the trial one day, and somehow he knew about Dad. He said, 'Gina, do you want to tell us anything about this?' And I said, 'I don't know.' And he said, 'Was he [Ruby] guilty?' And I said, 'I don't know.' 'Well, what happened to him?' 'I don't know.'

"So he ended up giving me detention, and said, 'I want you to go to the library and pull all these books, and give me a report.' And so I went to the library and I started seeing Dad's name. And I went back to [my teacher's] office, and I said, 'My dad's name is in these books!' And he said, 'OK, you can go home now, that's all I wanted you to do. I wanted you to realize how important it was. Now go home and talk to your dad about it.'"

A literate, thoughtful man, Causey was part of what several Dallas lawyers called the "smartest" jury they had ever seen in a murder case. Even flamboyant defense attorney Melvin Belli, the "King of Torts," said, in the superior fashion that infuriated many at the time (including some jurors): "I think the intelligence level of our jury is well above what you would expect from a cross section of Dallas residents" (Kaplan and Waltz 1965, 114). In a more generous (and less arch) moment, Belli offered, "They're an intelligent group of people, but they're all from Dallas. We would be happy with this jury if they were from any other city except Dallas, and in any other case but this one" (Richmond and Fenley 1964).

As Causey's time to be questioned by Belli arrived, he tried to reassure himself that surely he would not be selected. Max wrote:

> As I was seated in the witness box, I remember thinking that my three-and-one-half days waiting were up.

> If I were lucky in an hour or two at the most, I would
> certainly be found unacceptable as a juror and dismissed
> to return home to my family.

And so it is apparent that being selected as the first juror in the trial came as a tremendous shock to Causey, as he wrote: "In my thirty-five years on this planet I had never been exposed to a more devastating shock than at that moment. I suddenly felt as though the ceiling and all the upper seven floors of the building had collapsed on my head."

If the reader of Causey's memoir and diary is expecting splashy revelations, he or she will be disappointed. For this is the writing of a serious, cautious person, a man, like so many of his generation, with abundant respect for duty and authority. But Causey's writings are first-hand accounts of one of the most controversial, significant trials of the twentieth century, and reveal new insights into the dynamics of the jury and its deliberations:

> I admitted to the other jurors that I had voted for [a]
> life [sentence] and stated my reasons for so doing. . . .
> I was deliberately attempting to slow down what I felt
> was to be the ultimate sentence of death.

Four other Ruby jury members were interviewed for this book: Robert "Bob" Flechtner, Glenn Holton, J. Waymon Rose, and Doug Sowell. It is believed this is the first time that the jurors have commented at length on the trial since it ended more than thirty-five years ago. In reading the memoir and diary of Causey and interviewing Flechtner, Holton, Rose, and Sowell, one conclusion is inescapable: Belli set a very difficult task for himself in attempting to convince a Texas jury, in 1964, that Jack Ruby suffered from an exotic mental disease called psychomotor epilepsy, or the related psychomotor variant. Causey and the other jurors thought a defense that acknowledged Ruby's guilt but explained the killing in terms of his emotional reaction to the assassination of President Kennedy would have been much more convincing, and might have at least spared Ruby the death penalty. Max wrote:

In my layman's opinion, any good lawyer could have gotten Ruby off with something less than a death sentence if he had thrown Ruby on the mercy of the court and pleaded plain old 'temporary insanity' brought on by emotional stress over the loss of his beloved President.

Many observers, in the months leading up to the trial, believed a Dallas County jury would never be asked to decide Ruby's fate. It was widely assumed a change of venue would be granted. Even as the trial began, and some 900 prospective jurors were called to the court, defense counsel Belli still pushed for the trial to be moved. Belli had announced in December, two months earlier, that he would ask for a change of venue. But on the Friday before jury selection began, State District Judge Joe B. Brown put aside Belli's request to have the trial moved, declaring: "The true test of whether the state and defense can get a fair trial rests on the prospective jurors. The decision rests until examination of the jurors" (Kaplan and Waltz 1965, 77). At the beginning of the first day of testimony, Brown formally ruled against the defense's motion for a change of venue (Statement of Facts, 1). Brown's decision not to move the trial would eventually return to haunt him when a new trial was ordered two years later.

During the jury selection process, Belli attempted to show the trial should not be held in Dallas: "We prepared to show that it was impossible to find a fair jury in Dallas" (Belli 1964, 113). Belli believed that the citizenry of Dallas, embarrassed by the assassination of John F. Kennedy and then the televised murder of Kennedy's alleged assassin, Lee Harvey Oswald, would be eager to make a scapegoat of Ruby: "The man [Ruby] might have to be convicted in order to acquit the city" (Belli 1964, 106). He also called Dallas a "city of shame" after the trial (Belli 1964, 2). At one point during jury selection, Belli waved in the air a tabloid newspaper titled *The Thunderbolt—The White Man's Point of View*. It had been distributed in Dallas, he said, and it was "vile, the filthiest, nastiest thing I've ever seen." The paper was dated November 1963 and contained a story with the headline, "Kennedy Keeps Mistress." Belli declared, "We don't have that kind of filth in

California," and replying to a remark made in the "mild uproar" he had created in the courtroom, he said, "We didn't have the president assassinated in California" (Fenley 1964). Prospective jurors, other than the venireman being questioned, were not allowed in the courtroom to hear such outbursts, and had been admonished not to read the newspapers or listen to the news on radio and television, but before Belli learned the trial would not be moved from Dallas, he had seriously antagonized the community.

With an eye to a possible appeal, Belli used all of his fifteen peremptory challenges, plus three extra ones he was granted, to reject prospective jurors. Peremptory challenges allow an attorney to reject a juror without stating a reason. Belli wanted it to be shown on the record that it was very difficult to choose a Dallas County jury. In the end, after fourteen days, the attorneys examined 162 potential jurors, including those from a second group of fifty, before the final group of twelve was seated (Kaplan and Waltz 1965, 113).

The questioning of the jurors often was contentious. Prosecuting attorney Henry Wade asked prospective juror George A. Warren if he could impartially weigh the evidence in the case. Warren responded that he could come to a just decision, "or one you would consider just." At that, Belli leaped to his feet and denounced Warren's comment, saying it showed the "true unconscious feeling of Dallas." Later, the examination of Warren took a bitter, comical turn. "If it were proved that it was Jack Ruby who shot Oswald in the basement of city hall, would that be proof to you that he was guilty of the murder?" Belli asked Warren. "Wouldn't it to you?" shot back Warren. "No!" Belli shouted, and pleaded again with Judge Brown for a change of venue, which, of course, was denied. Warren was excused from jury service ("Dwindling Ruby Juror Pool" 1964). At one point, Belli's assistant, Joe Tonahill, a massive man from the Piney Woods of East Texas, was fined $25 for contempt of court when he snapped a pencil in two and threw the pieces on the floor, striking the judge's bench ("Defense Employs" 1964).

Of course, the Ruby trial was complicated by the fact that the murder of Oswald had been televised live to the entire country, and taped replays had been broadcast again and again. Very few people anywhere had not seen at least a playback of the shooting. Ruby's defense team bitterly complained that Judge Brown allowed those who had seen the shooting either live on in a replay to serve as jurors. Conflicting accounts of the trial say either ten or eleven of the twelve jurors had seen Ruby shoot Oswald on television. Max Causey saw the shooting in a televised replay.

Looking back at the newspaper coverage of the Jack Ruby trial more than thirty-five years later, it is striking that the individual jurors received so much publicity. Causey's selection as the first juror was front-page news, and several feature stories on him and his family followed, even giving their Garland address. Similar stories were written on the other jurors. Even as the trial was proceeding, Causey recognized the dangerous nature of the publicity:

> All of this publicity that we were getting was a little exciting but it was far more frightening. Everyone concerned with the security of the jury felt that no good could possibly come from this much exposure of the jury to the public. Later on, many of us were to better understand this.

This is the cauldron into which twelve exceptional and ordinary people were thrown in the winter of 1964, just three months after the public murder of a charismatic young president literally around the corner, followed two days later by the televised killing of his apparent assassin. In the following pages, this significant page of history is presented through the eyes of one of the trial's central characters—Max Causey, the foreman of the jury.

J. M. Dempsey

(top left) Jack Ruby immediately after his arrest, Nov. 24, 1963

(bottom left) Jack Ruby, center, examines documents with defense attorneys Joe Tonahill, left, and Melvin Belli before a pretrial hearing.

(right) Jack Ruby and defense attorney Melvin Belli swarmed by the media, Feb. 10, 1964

(below) Before the start of the trial Feb. 10, 1964, prosecuting attorneys Henry Wade (foreground) and Bill Alexander meet the press, with defense attorney Joe Tonahill and Jack Ruby visible in the background.

All photographs courtesy *Fort Worth Star-Telegram* Photograph Collection, Special Collections Division, The University of Texas at Arlington Libraries.

(right) Judge Joe B. Brown

(below) Prosecuting attorneys Bill Alexander (left) and Henry Wade

Photographs courtesy *Fort Worth Star-Telegram* Photograph Collection, Special Collections Division, The University of Texas at Arlington Libraries.

Section I

Diary

February 20, 1964, to March 14, 1964

By Max Causey

Editor's Note: On the morning after he was selected as the first juror in the trial of Jack Ruby, Max Causey sat down at the long table in the jury deliberation room with a stenographer's pad. Somewhat calmer than he had been the previous afternoon, he began to write about his feelings on suddenly being thrust into the maelstrom that had begun with the assassination of John F. Kennedy three months before. He wrote mostly with a pencil in a neat, precise fashion that reflected his methodical manner. He wrote extensively about his personal feelings, but relatively little about his thoughts on the trial itself. Those thoughts are much more evident in the memoir that he wrote after the trial, based on the diary. The memoir appears after the diary in this book. The diary is presented here as a first-hand account of the Jack Ruby trial as it unfolded, with virtually no changes from Causey's original writing. Parenthetical phrases are Causey's; information in brackets was added by the editor. Editor's notes are in bold.

Max Causey

[Thursday,] 20 February 1964   11:25 A.M.

I was called to the courtroom and was seated in the box. D. A. Wade questioned me on capital punishment in proven 1st-degree murder cases. After approx. 20 min. of questioning, the state accepted me as a juror. At this time (11:45 A.M.) Judge Brown recessed for lunch. I was admonished about discussing the case and released without restraint until 1:45 P.M. I had two hours for lunch but no appetite, so I walked the several blocks from the courthouse to midtown where I entered the Eatwell Restaurant on Main Street and ordered a bowl of tomato soup and a glass of ice tea. By the time I had finished the lunch it was 12:45 P.M., still an hour to kill.

Dallas weather that particular Thursday was exceptionally nice for a February afternoon. The temperature at noon was in the upper fifties, a bit nippy in the shade but pleasantly comfortable in the warm sunlight. As I now look back on that leisurely walk back to the courthouse, I recall stopping many times to gaze into the window displays along Main Street, looking but not really seeing that which was displayed. My mind was preoccupied, contemplating what it would be like when I again stepped inside the courtroom upon the stand where the defense would try to disqualify me as a juror.

Many thoughts went through my mind, the most recurring one was that I must not allow myself to become confused or mixed up when I face the rapid fire questions of the chief defense counsel, Mr. Melvin Belli. All I intended to do was to state the truth of what I had seen, heard and read since Nov. 24, 1963 regarding the case. However, I felt certain that no matter how careful I was with my answers that some time during my examination that I would become mixed up or confused on some minor legal technicality that would disqualify me as a juror on the case. This was not poor reasoning on my part since 23 prospective jurors had gone the route and not one juror had yet been accepted. I certainly didn't have any desire to serve on this jury and as I absently gazed into a Sanger-Harris display window 2 blocks east of the Courthouse, I told myself that on this fact I really need not worry, that the defense would find reason to strike me from qualification as they had the previous 23. (I was no. 26, but nos. 21 and 25 had previously been excused by Judge Joe Brown prior to qualification questioning.)

Having reassured myself that I would not really be found qualified (or acceptable) by the defense, I glanced at my watch for probably the hundredth time in the past two hours. It was 1:20 P.M.: twenty-five more minutes. I returned to the courthouse, rode the elevator up to the sixth floor where I used the restroom (this was the only restroom I had located). I checked my appearance in the mirror to make certain my lunch wasn't showing and strolled back to the elevator which carried me back to the first floor. From here I walked out the south door and re-entered the building at the other south entrance which allowed entrance to the stairway that led up to the courtroom. The stairway was packed with newsmen and spectators. I elbowed my way to the top of the stairs where I asked a uniformed deputy sheriff where I should wait the next ten minutes, and he escorted me through the crowd and into the courtroom.

It was 1:50 P.M.; my three-and-one-half days of waiting were up. If I were lucky in an hour or two at the most, I would certainly be disqualified as a juror and dismissed to return home to my family where I would assume my regular routine. The defense lawyer who questioned me was Mr. M. Belli, but not at all like what I had expected. I was not ill at ease under his questioning. He was courteous, charming and eloquently smooth. The questioning was thorough and deliberate (It is not my intent to disclose any questions or facts pertinent to the case in this article.) As Mr. Belli asked question after question, and I in turn answered between frequent objections by the state (Mr. Jim Bowie), it became increasingly apparent to me that thus far I had not given an answer that I felt justified my disqualification, which I still felt was a certainty.

My juror qualification questioning by the defense continued for approximately one hour. At about 2:50 P.M., Mr. Belli asked Judge Brown if he (the defense) was to be allowed more than the prescribed 15 inexcusable strikes [peremptory challenges], to which Judge Brown answered something to the effect that he could not foresee this possibility. The defense lawyers then went into a whispered conference. I was very uncomfortable but still I expected Mr. Belli to use his strike prerogative to delete me as a juror. After a three- or four-minute conference, Mr. Belli rose to his feet and passed the juror qualification acceptance back to Mr. Wade. Mr. Wade rose to his feet and stated that the state would accept me as a juror. He then sat down. Mr. Belli again rose to his feet. He stated that the defense had no real objection to me as a juror and that I was acceptable.

In my thirty-five years on this planet, I have never been exposed to a more devastating shock than at that moment. I suddenly felt as though the ceiling and all the upper seven floors of the building had collapsed on my head. The next thing I remember was Judge Brown speaking to me, to swear me in with the oath of a juror. I remember trying to stand erect but Judge Brown allowed me to remain seated for the oath, and considering my real shock of the moment, this was indeed a kind gesture.

The juror's oath was administered to me and the Court Bailiff, Mr. Bo Mabra, quickly escorted me through a locked door immediately behind the judge's bench, up a winding fight of stairs to a large suite which was to be used as the jury deliberation room. This was to be my daily habitat during the many days ahead, while downstairs the long, slow deliberate jury qualification continued in the quest for the other eleven jurors. As I climbed those winding stairs that first time, I remember asking the bailiff a question which I really knew the answer to, but I had to hear it from him: Was I the first juror? Of course, his answer was in the affirmative. The bailiff made me as comfortable as a man in my present state of mind could be. He hurriedly returned to the courtroom, locking the massive door at the foot of the stairs. The locked door served a dual role; one was to keep anyone from approaching me, the other was to restrain me if need be.

Not until the bailiff left me alone for the first time did the full momentous impact of what was happening to me begin to settle over me as a choking, smothering *shroud*. Suddenly it was frightfully painful to ponder the many aspects of my personal situation. My first concern was how this would affect my wonderful family. How would they cope with all the family problems that I had thus far always handled? There were so many, many financial problems that needed my guidance in order to remain in the black. My wife is a very remarkable woman, intelligent, lovable, and understanding, but in all our 10½ years of married life, I and I alone had administered our family affairs. We often discussed our financial status vs. our needs and desires, but ultimately the responsibility of the final decision had always been mine. How could she now react to these added responsibilities? Could she cope with all the little family crises that arise from day to day? In short, could she be the mother and father to the family for an extended period?

What about my employer, Ling-Temco-Vought? This was a grave concern to me although the firm encouraged all its employees to serve their civic responsibilities such as serving on jury duty when summoned. The company very generously paid our salaries while we served on jury duty, but for how long? Who could foresee an employee being assigned confining jury duty which could conceivably last weeks? Would my pay continue through a prolonged trial? If not, my financial situation would become crucial very shortly. Unfortunately, our checking account could not withstand the omission of even one bimonthly paycheck. The financial drain of a large home mortgage, new car payments, doctor bills, insurance and other family expenses required a delicate balancing of the budget. Also my duties with the company had just suddenly become critical due to the receipt of a new classified contract to which I was to have the responsibility of planning, scheduling and cost control. In my absence, the job would surely be given to someone else and where would this leave me?

I could continue exploring the many troubled thoughts I experienced during that first afternoon but to do so would perhaps bring boredom to the reader and definitely bring pain to my mind. In between fleeting worried thoughts, I paced the floor within the confinement of my habitat, glancing so many, many times at my watch only to find that a few seconds had elapsed since I last checked the dial. This climatic afternoon dragged laboriously on until 5:30 when the bailiff returned. At the head of the stairs just outside my suite, he greeted me with, "Hey, Max, have you jumped out a window yet?" It wasn't really funny but I forced a laugh as I returned the greeting. It was wonderful to have someone's company again after 2½ hours of pondering the situation.

The next hour was spent in familiarizing me with my sleeping quarters. These were far short of the comforts of home but fully adequate for their purpose. The bedroom was about 7 feet by 7 feet with a single built-in, comfortable bunk bed, lavatory and commode. There was a shaving mirror over the lavatory. A tiled shower was next door to my room. The bailiff slept just across the hall. His room was a carbon copy of mine with the exception of a telephone. This telephone was our emergency link with the outside world. Although I was at no time allowed to talk to anyone over this phone, it was some comfort to know that it was there in the event that an emergency should arise within my family. The bailiff called my wife to inform her that I was to be detained for awhile. He gave her his phone no. for use in emergency situations.

At about 7 P.M. the bailiff suggested we go out to dinner. I welcomed the thought of getting out in the open but I didn't feel hungry. We stepped out of the courthouse into the cold, damp and dark night, as a fast-moving cold front had engulfed Dallas since I had been out at lunch. We walked the three blocks to the Dallas-Jefferson Hotel on Houston Street where we ordered dinner. The food, under any other circumstances I'm sure would have been delicious, but I could only pick at it. I had no desire for food at that time. We returned to our sleeping quarters at about 8 P.M. By this time, my wife had brought the luggage that I required for a prolonged stay. The luggage was left at the sheriff's office where we picked it up.

Bo Mabra (the bailiff) and I talked awhile and very soon I found that he was a very friendly, considerate and likable person, ideally suited for his job. He was to be my nursemaid, den mother, chaplain, doctor and most important, my only link to the world beyond for the days ahead. Bo had held this same job for 8 years during which time he had played nursemaid to many such jury panels. It was old stuff to Bo. We drank coffee and discussed the prospects of how long our confinement might last. Our most optimistic estimate was three weeks. Neither of us dared to predict how much longer it would take once the jury was finally picked to hear all the evidence in court and reach a decision as to the innocence or guilt of Mr. Ruby.

I went to bed that first night contemplating what lay ahead. I wondered who might be the 2nd juror, how long would it take to pick him (or her), would it take as long to get the 2nd as it had to get me. If so, I would surely be alone for three or four more days of questioning. With a Sunday falling during the period, this would indicate that I likely would not have another juror companion until Monday or Tuesday. As I now lay in bed, my mind raced over and over again all the thoughts that I first entertained when I realized I had been accepted. But now in the darkness additional would-be problems kept cropping up. My mind kept cycling and recycling until I mercifully lapsed into unconsciousness. I slept fitfully until 3 A.M., at which time I looked at my watch and thought, Would this night never end? For the next 3 hours, I frequently catnapped, waking up each time thinking that it was all a bad dream. At last, I heard Bo in the shower next door to my room. Thank heaven it was morning.

My second day started with my shaving and a quick shower. By the time I had dressed, Bo had brought coffee down from the jail kitchen so we enjoyed a cup before departing outside for our breakfast. As we left the courthouse, the press and spectators had already begun to assemble with still two hours before the court was to reconvene in the jury selection. As we stepped out onto the street, it was bitter cold. Snow had sprinkled the autos that were parked on the street. An occasional snowflake still fluttered from a dark overcast sky.

Just outside the courthouse door was a newsstand. As we strolled by I could not help but observe that I had made the front page. I was not allowed to read the newspaper but I did see my wife and older son's picture on the front page. I had not anticipated being such a newsworthy item. I wondered how my wife had reacted to such instant publicity, [because] she was not the type to seek it in the least.

The breakfast of sweet roll and coffee was concluded and we returned to the courthouse up the stairway through the throng, into the courtroom, up the stairs to my day quarters, where my long wait was to be resumed. While waiting on this second day, I decided to make notes, or a daily log of activities. This seemed like an excellent way of spending my time.

At 11:45, Bo returned and suggested that it would be better if we stayed in the room for lunch, since he had received word that the press was waiting on the street exit for photographs or questioning, which was not allowed by the court. So, to avoid the possibility of a disturbance, I agreed that sandwiches brought up to the room would be fine with me. As we ate the sandwiches, I pumped Bo for information regarding the no. of prospective jurors that had been rejected during the morning, and who rejected them. I was very interested in whether the jurors were disqualified by Judge Brown or whether they were struck by either the state or the defense. My interest here was justified since I knew both the state and defense each had only 15 strikes. This is to say that both the state and defense could reject 15 prospective jurors each on peremptory challenges without stating any reason. Any prospective juror that did not qualify in the judge's own opinion, he could strike without it being charged either to the state or the defense. My reasoning was simple mathematics. I knew that the defense had already struck 5 when I was accepted. This left them with 10 remaining strikes and over 100 prospective jurors yet to be examined. The more strikes used by the state or defense reduced the remaining strikes; consequently, when they ran out, assuming the court did not grant additional strikes, the sooner either the defense or the state would have to start accepting jurors.

While Bo and I munched on cold corned beef sandwiches, Bo told me that during the morning session the defense had used up two more of its peremptory challenges, the state had used two and Judge Brown had disqualified two. The box score was now 34 prospects questioned, and one selected. The state had used two strikes (peremptory challenges) and the defense had used seven.

With lunch recess over, Bo returned to the courtroom. I tried to kill time by playing solitaire. After numerous failures to beat "sol," I had just given up, when I heard the lock turn on the massive door at the foot of the stairs and the noise of the excitement in the court filtered up the stairs. I heard footsteps. This time it was evidently more noise than Bo had usually made each time he visited me. Excitement swelled within me as I anticipated company. I was really in luck. Not only was Bo bringing me a companion, but I quickly recognized him as one of the prospective jurors whom I had lunched with only two days ago. Mr. Allen W. McCoy was the second acceptable juror. I quickly greeted him with a warm handshake and a hot cup of coffee. My "solitaire" wait was over. I looked at my watch. It was 3:55 P.M. After 25 hours, I now had a companion to share my waiting.

I explained to Allen what I knew about our day quarters, our night quarters and the daily routine which we would pursue while we waited for no. 3. It was apparent that Allen was not as shocked upon his selection as I had been with mine. He seemed to quickly accept the role that had been dealt him and just as quickly accepted the routine which accompanied it.

Allen and I talked and the next 1½ hours passed swiftly. At 5:30, Bo returned (alone this time) and we proceeded to our night quarters where Allen was acquainted with the other side of our routine. At 7:00 P.M., Bo carried us out to dinner. This was the first time in about 36 hours that I felt hungry. After dinner, we walked around for about 20 min. and returned to our night quarters. We talked and read magazines until around 11 P.M. when we each returned to our separate rooms and beds.

The following day was Sat. and was to be a regular working day for the court. We awoke at 6 A.M. anxious for the day to start, being optimistic about a quicker selection of the jurors. After breakfast, we once again climbed the 20 steps in back of the judge's bench in the courtroom and arrived at our day quarters. Our earlier optimism suffered a setback at approx. 12:30 P.M. when Bo returned from the courtroom, stating that Judge Brown had recessed until 9 A.M. Monday. No additional jurors had been accepted, so McCoy and I along with our bailiff faced a day and one-half of waiting during which time there was no possibility of any progress being made on the jury selection. This was to be my first weekend away from my family in over eight years. I wasn't looking forward to this separation. However, it didn't turn out to be as bad as I had expected, thanks to our very thoughtful bailiff. Bo had parked his car in a lot nearby and he said that he had asked Sheriff [Bill] Decker if we could drive out to suburban restaurants for our meals during this 1½-day court recess. Permission was granted. This was a welcome break in the monotony of our daily routine and it helped pass the long weekend. We had two such meals out, Sat. lunch and Sunday dinner.

Monday, 24 February 1964

The second week of jury selection. Allen and I were eager for the court to resume its juror questioning. We wanted to see some progress made in the selection of jurors. Approximately 11:15, we heard the door at the foot of the stairs being opened and two sets of footsteps were heard coming up the stairs. Bo was bringing us our third juror. Juror number 3 was Mrs. Mildred McCollum of Garland. She was the first lady juror accepted. With the acceptance of a lady on the jury, it was required that a lady bailiff, Mrs. Nell Tyler, be assigned to keep her company and take care of her needs as Bo was doing for the men. Our number now included 5 when we went out for lunch, including the two bailiffs. During our lunch walk, our photographs were taken for the first time since our selection. Judge Brown had warned the press that no pictures would be allowed. We never knew when this picture was taken. However, we saw it in the Tue. morning *Dallas Morning News*. Monday night, the five of us, Allen, Mildred, the two bailiffs and I, went out to eat dinner in a group. The first day of the second week of jury selection had ended with three jurors selected.

Tuesday, 25 February 1964

Today we believed would be a profitable day in the jury selection. We were correct. At approximately 10:30, we heard the familiar footsteps on the stairs. We were introduced to juror no. 4, Mr. Gene Dickerson of Mesquite. We poured him a cup of coffee and filled him in on jury life as we knew it. Within the next hour and before lunch we were privileged to welcome juror no. 5, Mr. Doug Sowell of Dallas, Oak Cliff. At noon our number including the two bailiffs was 7 and the news photographers had a ball while we walked the 4 blocks to lunch at the Dallas Jefferson Hotel. The photographers were everywhere, even in the dining room snapping pictures while we ate lunch. The two jurors selected during Tue. morning were all for that day. Tue. night the five of us and the two bailiffs piled into Bo's car and went out to the Flight Deck Restaurant for dinner. The change of scenery did wonders for our morale.

Wednesday, 26 February 1964

With each passing day, we grew in number and in anxiety for the 12th man. His coming would surely bring a cheer from each of us. At approximately 10:20, we heard the familiar ring of footsteps on the stairs and Bo brought us juror no. 6. He was R. J. (Bob) Flechtner of Richardson. He was followed at 11:45 by juror no. 7, Mrs. Gwen English, who qualified about 11:30.

The news photographers were set for us at lunch. They climbed up posts, stood on top of cars, mailboxes and any available object in order to photograph the 7 jurors. After lunch, we settled down in our day quarters to await for juror number 8. We didn't have to wait long. At about 3 P.M., Mr. Glenn Holton took up his position as juror no. 8. This had been the best day for jury selection. Three jurors had been selected and the defense used one peremptory challenge. They had only four left. The state had used five challenges and the defense eleven. Wednesday night, we had dinner at Vincent's Seafood Restaurant. We were taking shape, finally.

Thursday, 27 February 1964

After breakfast at Malendorf's, we returned to our day quarters to wait for juror no. 9. We were still waiting at lunch. The defense had used one more strike during the morning, challenge no. 12. We looked ahead eagerly for additions to our number. Our luck wasn't all bad this day. About 5 P.M. we cheered the arrival of Mr. Jim Cunningham, juror no. 9. Thursday ended with 9 jurors selected. The defense had now used 13 challenges.

Friday, 28 February 1964

Today we had only one addition to our number. He was Wayman Rose of Dallas, the no. 10 juror.

Saturday, 29 February 1964

We were very apprehensive about filling the jury today. However, Judge Brown recessed at noon with no jurors picked during the morning. We looked forward to a long weekend locked up in our rooms unable to get out. This was my second weekend to be locked up. It was good news when we learned that both state and defense lawyers had agreed for us to have a TV in our lounge room, but news and certain other programs were censored. This helped our time to pass faster, but even so it was a long weekend. I was really missing my family by this time.

Monday, 2 March 1964

Today starts the 3rd week of jury selection and it is my 11th day to be locked up. I never realized before so completely the meaning of freedom. However, it is not the 11 days just passed that causes me concern. It is the many long days ahead during the selection of the two [remaining] jurors and the trial itself that I fear. Monday, 2 March passes without another juror being selected. This was my worst day since the day I was accepted. The time period to conclude this entire affair may exceed my worst fears. We now have gone through 2 days of questioning since juror no. 10 was chosen on Friday.

This group of jurors is outstanding. The intelligence level is well above that of the average jury. So far, everyone has been very congenial, and considerate of each other. We have a good cross-section from all walks of life. The personalities of a couple are such that the morale of the group is kept high through joking and witticisms. We joke about how long the trial will take with what we hope is vast exaggeration, anything for a laugh. For the most part, everyone is holding up as well as could be expected under the circumstances. We know that we may be free and easy with our joking now, but once we have heard the judge's charge to us at the end of the trial and we start our deliberation, all joking will end and the seriousness of the situation will dominate our every thought.

Tuesday, 3 March 1964

There is a general letdown feeling throughout our number in regard to a quick selection of jurors no. 11 and 12. We feel like it may be the end of the week before we have our 12th juror. The state has now used 11 strikes and the defense has used all 18 of their allocated strikes [including the three additional peremptory challenges allowed by Judge Brown]. The defense must now rely upon offending a prospective juror they don't want since they must make him angry and cause the judge to strike him. This type of questioning is very time consuming. We are not at all apprehensive [optimistic] about a fast end to these filibustering tactics.

The Tue. morning newspaper was cut to ribbons indicating much fireworks in yesterday's session. We know that it got noisy because at times we could hear shouting and objections all the way up to our day quarters. We can only speculate as to what is going on. It bothers us only from the curiosity standpoint and how this probable delay is accepted by our families and employers.

Editor's Note: On Monday, March 2, Belli erupted when a representative of the National Epilepsy League distributed a "Fact Sheet on Epilepsy" to newsmen. The literature called into question the defense's use of the mental illness psychomotor epilepsy in Ruby's defense. "You don't have to worry too much about a patient in a psychomotor seizure," it said. "You will read in novels and see in the movies all kinds of dramatizations, [and] spiced-up stories about what psychomotor epileptics do: murders, criminal activities, etc. This is nonsense. A large sample of the prison population of Massachusetts was studied and not one epileptic was found."

Ironically, the person quoted in the document was Dr. Frederic A. Gibbs, a member of the league's advisory board. The defense hung

much of its hopes on Dr. Gibbs' reading of Ruby's brain wave patterns, which he said showed evidence that Ruby suffered from psychomotor epilepsy. Dr. Gibbs became the final witness to testify for the defense in the trial. Belli angrily moved for a mistrial, on the grounds that the remaining prospective jurors could see information about the fact sheet in the newspaper. Belli also apparently believed there had been an attempt to distribute the literature to the potential jurors. After much debate, including what was reported by an enterprising reporter who was somehow allowed into the room as a profane and raucous session in the judge's chambers, Brown rejected Belli's motions for a mistrial and a change of venue (Kaplan and Waltz, 1965, 110–111).

This day closed with jubilation. We were rewarded with juror no. 11, Mrs. Aileen Shields about 10:30 A.M. She joined us for lunch. The most important juror of all, juror no. 12, Mrs. Louise Malone, joined us at 2:30 P.M. She was welcomed with as heavy applause as 11 anxious jurors could muster. Morale soared to its highest peak since before my selection. Each of us felt that at long last we would get the opportunity to serve in the position to which we had been so carefully selected. We were told by Bo Mabra that the trial would begin promptly at 9 A.M. Wednesday morning. This momentous occasion called for a dinner celebration. A vote was taken and we decide to go to Kirby's Steak House for dinner.

Prior to going out to dinner we all went up to our night quarters to clean up and wait for the 6 P.M. departure time. We planned our departure to dinner by unmarked sheriff's cars to avoid the news photographers who we knew were waiting out on the streets for the first photos of the complete jury. Not even the deputy sheriffs who drove the three cars knew where we were going for dinner until we were driving away from the courthouse. Judge Brown had instructed that no photos of the jury would be taken.

Wednesday, 4 March 1964

We are supposed to start hearing testimony today. However, we don't expect to occupy our seats before lunch due to all the anticipated motions and etc. After breakfast we returned to our day quarters, made a pot of coffee and began our wait to be called downstairs into the jury box.

We got our chance today to sit in the jury box for the very first time. We heard about 1 hour and 50 min. of testimony this A.M. During the afternoon, we heard about 3 hours of testimony. The trial was really getting under way now.

Thursday, 5 March 1964

Testimony lasted about 2 hours this morning and about 3 hours this afternoon.

Friday, 6 March 1964

Testimony started at 10 A.M. Bo Mabra told me as I came down the stairs to the jury box that my wife was in the audience and where she was seated. I quickly spotted her sitting there. This was the first time I had seen her in 15 days or about 363 hours. Of course, I could not speak to her but our eyes met several times during the day when there were frequent delays and pauses in the testimony. The state concluded its testimony shortly after lunch. The defense started its parade of witnesses before us at 3:00 P.M.

Judge Brown dealt the jury a devastating morale blow at 4:45 P.M. when he announced that court would recess until 9 A.M. Monday morning. We the jury wanted the court to operate on Sat., as well as longer hours during the day with shorter recesses.

We now faced a long tiresome weekend locked up. This was my third such weekend without my freedom. For most of the jurors, all but Allen and myself, it was their second weekend. However, for two jurors, nos. 11 and 12, it was their first such weekend. This weekend was spent just loafing around our quarters. Nearly everyone slept until 8 or 9 A.M. By 10 A.M. Sat. morning we were all up and hungry enough to walk the 3 blocks to the Dallas Jefferson Coffee Shop for breakfast. With breakfast leisurely concluded, we returned to our quarters around 11:30 A.M. That afternoon, Bo took some of the men out for haircuts. I didn't go this time since I had received a haircut the previous Sat. Sat. evening we were carried out to dinner. Sunday's activity was almost a carbon copy of Sat. except we stood on the street in back of the

Dallas Hotel and watched a wrecking crane demolish a building. We all stood and watched this activity for more than an hour. We all enjoyed this very much.

Monday, 9 March 1964

A day of courtroom testimony. We had asked Bo to speak to Judge Brown about speeding things up by shorter recesses and longer days. The judge really cooperated. We didn't shut down until 6:45 P.M. It was a good day for the jury (measured in hours of testimony heard).

Tuesday, 10 March 1964

Today, as we walked away from the courtroom for lunch, we saw several persons in front of the courthouse carrying pickets. We could not read the pickets from our distant sighting. I remember thinking that it takes all kinds of people to make up the population of a city the size of Dallas, but why do some people want to show off like "nuts"? We had a fairly good day in court. Not as good as Monday, but we didn't shut down today until 5:45 P.M.

Wednesday, 11 March 1964

This is my 21st day in captivity with no contact (personal) with my dear family. I wondered how much longer it would be. My best guess was 8 or ten more working days in court. We were shocked early, 9:30 A.M., when the defense rested its case. The state started its rebuttal at about 10:45 A.M. and rested its rebuttal at about 5 P.M. The defense started its rebuttal about 5 P.M. We recessed for the day at 5:45 P.M.

Thursday, 12 March 1964

My 22nd day as a juror. The defense rested their rebuttal at 12:15 and we recessed for lunch until 1:45 P.M. The state started its closing rebuttal at 1:45 and closed its case at 5 P.M. The defense started its final rebuttal. We recessed for the day at about 6 P.M.

Friday, 13 March 1964

My 23rd day. It is an apprehensive jury that fills the box today. Judge Brown told us yesterday that the court intended to finish this case before the day (Friday) ends. We expect to have the charge and start our deliberation tonight.

Judge Brown read the charge to us tonight. He started about 8:15 and finished about 8:35. The lawyers started their final appeals [arguments] to the jury shortly before 8:45 P.M. We heard first from Mr. Alexander for the state. We listened to all seven lawyers, four for the state and three for the defense. Judge Brown had allowed each side 2½ hours for the appeal. Finally, at 1:15 Saturday morning, 14 March, Mr. Wade closed out the appeals and the trial. The rest was up to the jury. Judge Brown asked us if we wanted to start our deliberation then or retire and start deliberations the next (Sat.) morning. We agreed to retire for the night.

Saturday, 14 March 1964

We arose around 7:30 and proceeded to breakfast by about 8:30. By 9:00 A.M. we had finished breakfast and returned to the deliberation room. While I was in the restroom, the rest of the jury elected me foreman. However, I wouldn't accept this election and a new election was held. Again, I was elected foreman. I suppose it was my seniority that drew this honor. After two hours and twenty minutes (11:20 A.M.), we had agreed unanimously on a verdict. I walked down the familiar 20 steps to the foot of the stairs and knocked on the door. Quickly, Bo Mabra opened the door and I told him we had reached a verdict. He told me he would have to call the judge to the courtroom.

It was approximately 45 minutes before the court could assemble to hear our verdict. At approximately 12:15, we were seated in the jury box for the last time. Judge Brown asked if we had reached a verdict, and we answered or nodded affirmatively. Then, Bo came over and I handed him the charge, which had been filled in and signed by me. We all looked at the defendant as the judge read the verdict aloud to the court. "We the jury find the defendant guilty of murder with malice and affix his punishment at death." There was no visible emotional change in the defendant. He was ushered out by the deputies and immediately Mr. Belli was screaming like a wild man. Pandemonium broke loose in the courtroom. The cameramen climbed the walls to get shots and microphones up to Mr. Belli and others to Mr. Wade. Simultaneous with this pandemonium, Judge Brown was dismissing us and thanking us for the service we rendered as jurors.

Bo ushered us up the stairs to wait in the deliberation room for the last time while some of the excitement in the courtroom subsided. In approximately 15 min. we made our last exit down the so familiar 20 stairs and out of the deliberation room. We returned to our night quarters and finished packing for home. Everyone was eager to get home and to see their loved ones again. We took turns on Bo's phone calling our families. When I called my wife it was the first time in 24 days that I had been allowed to talk directly to her. It was wonderful to hear her voice and be able to speak to her.

Sheriff Decker had suggested that his deputies drive us home since there was a huge mob completely surrounding the Records Building, everyone wanting pictures of the jury, some agreeing and others disagreeing with our verdict. As we left the building for the last time, the crowd outside was lined along the street, watching a parade. As the sheriff's car pulled out of the prisoner-unloading dock on the west side of the Records Building to enter Houston Street, for just an instant we were facing, not 50 yards away, the scene where on 22 Nov. 1963 this entire unbelievable episode of world history had first begun to unfold. In slightly less than four months, enough world-shaking history had been made to fill volumes of history books. The world would long remember the past 4 months: The argumentative speculation regarding the president's assassination, the assassination of his assassin, and the trial of Jack Ruby, the man who assassinated the assassin after he had been arrested and was in the custody of law enforcement officers.

No matter how historians reflect on the events of the past four months, whether history commends this verdict or condemns it, only time will tell, but as for me, my mark (insignificant as it may be) is niched in history. My "Trial of a Juror" is finished.

[Epilogue]

Trial by jury is one of the rights endowed upon each citizen by the Constitution. For nearly 200 years, it has been the accepted way of meting out justice in our courts of law. During this span of time, our society has made gigantic advancements in scientific and technical fields.

Many people feel that our legal and sociological fields have not kept pace with our scientific and technical advancements.

I would not attempt to become involved in such a discussion, but of one thing I am certain, and that is I know of no fairer method of rendering justice than our ancient trial-by-jury right.

Many times during these many days have I asked myself, "Why me, why did I allow myself to be accepted for this jury?" Several times during my qualification questioning I could have answered either the state or the defense in such a manner as to have had the court disqualify me as a juror. Why, then, did I not do this? The answer is simple. I could not do so without sacrificing those legal and moral aspects of our society that I hold most reverent.

The first question I asked myself, when I first became aware that I was to be a prospective juror on this case, was: Would I truly make the kind of juror that I would most like to have if I were the one on trial instead of Mr. Ruby, and would I be equally as fair to the state? I searched my heart and soul for an answer and felt beyond a doubt that I could, if asked to, render a completely fair and impartial verdict based solely on the facts presented in the courtroom, nothing less, nothing more.

I have been asked why I believe in capital punishment. This is a difficult question to answer, since I would really prefer that an easier and more humane method of major crime deterrent could be found. No past civilization has ever endured that didn't at some time enforce the death penalty on members of its society who committed crimes of varying degrees within its civilized framework.

I have never relished the thought of having the awful responsibility of sitting in judgment of another man's life. It is not something that I find easy to do, but I feel it is a moral and civic responsibility to do so. I am, whether I like it or not, a member of this society which is governed by man-made laws. The law states that when a duly accepted jury panel of 12 citizens finds beyond a reasonable doubt that a man is guilty of committing an unprovoked act of murder, with full and complete sanity, then he is subject to being sentenced to die for his crime. This law is upheld by the rule of the majority of the members of our society. Many people who agree with this law will, when summoned as a prospective juror on such a case, refuse to accept the responsibility of enforcing the law on moral or religious grounds. It is to these people that I appeal: Please do not condemn those of us in our society who feel that until such a time as a more humane and befitting deterrent to major crimes can be devised, our existing law must be enforced if our society is to survive.

I personally believe that when 12 God-fearing jurors seek to sit in judgment on a man's life, that each and every one should seek God's divine guidance in seeing that justice prevails.

WFAA-TV reporter Art Sinclair interviews Max Causey following the death of Jack Ruby, 1967. From the collection of Max and Rosemary Causey.

Section II

Memoir

"The Trial of a Juror"

By Max Causey

Editor's Note: Within one or two years of the end of the Ruby trial, Max Causey sat at a typewriter and wrote a memoir based upon the precisely printed diary he kept in a stenographer's notebook during the trial. The memoir is much more expansive than the diary; for example, Causey makes revealing comments on the crucial testimony of defense witness Dr. Frederic Gibbs in the memoir, but not in the diary. Also, his description of the jury deliberations is quite detailed in the memoir, but almost nonexistent in the diary.

We have expanded upon Causey's memoir with notes taken from the trial transcripts, newspaper articles, books, and other sources. Otherwise, his original writing has been left virtually untouched, with only minor editorial changes. Words that appear in parentheses are Causey's; words that appear in brackets are the editor's. Editor's notes are set off from the main text in boldface to distinguish them from Causey's writings.

Max Causey in 1967. From the collection of Max and Rosemary Causey.

During the second week of February 1964, I received a summons for Petit Jury duty. I was instructed to report to the Central Jury Room of the Dallas County Records building at 9:00 A.M. on 17 February 1964. At first, the only particular significance that I attached to this summons was that it was the first I had ever received for jury duty. It was soon called to my attention that this was the jury panel that was being summoned for the Jack Ruby trial. I read in the papers that some 900 summons had been mailed out. Since there were so many prospective jurors to select only twelve from, I practically dismissed the thought of being selected as one of the jurors for the Ruby trial. I told my wife that I would most likely sit on one of the civil cases that were also on the docket for that panel.

On the morning of 17 February, I reported to the Central Jury Room as instructed. Here along with the other 900 prospective jurors, I was welcomed by several judges who gave us short speeches on the honor and duty of serving our county and state by serving as jurors. This ceremony lasted for about an hour, at which time we were told that 150 names would be drawn and assigned to the court of Judge Joe Brown. Judge Brown, we all knew, had been assigned to hear the Ruby case.

I was the twenty-sixth name that was called out to report to Judge Brown's court. This still didn't really disturb me since I was only one out of the 150 that the twelve jurors were to be selected from. We all assembled in Judge Brown's borrowed courtroom where he told us that we were, from that moment on, not to read any articles, or watch television, or listen to the radio regarding anything about the Jack Ruby trial. Numbers one through ten were held for the remainder of the day and the rest of us were dismissed until 9:00 A.M. the next morning.

At home that night, I told my wife that there was still very little chance that I would be called to serve on the Ruby jury. That night I refrained from watching any news reports on television, nor did I read anything in the evening newspaper except the sports and comic sections.

During breakfast that first Tuesday morning, I told my wife that I didn't know how fast the jury would be selected but I felt reasonably certain that I wouldn't be questioned during the day.

When I reached the waiting room on the sixth floor of the Criminal Courts Building, I learned that no prospective jurors had been questioned during the previous day. The first ten of the prospective jurors had been allowed to go home shortly after the rest of us had been released. About 9:30 A.M., the first ten panelists were ordered down to Judge Brown's court, or rather just outside the courtroom to await their separate call-in to be questioned, one by one. About 10:30 A.M. all the prospective jurors, except the first fifty, were released for the remainder of the day. This did not include me, as I was number twenty-six. Finally at about 2:30 P.M. numbers twenty-one through fifty were also released for the day, including me.

By Wednesday morning 19 February, it was obvious that the jury selection was going to be a tediously long drawn-out affair. For me this day's schedule was almost a carbon copy of the previous day. At the close of the day, not one juror had yet been selected.

Wednesday night, I continued to refrain from reading or watching on TV anything pertaining to the Ruby trial. About five minutes past 10 P.M., my telephone rang and I answered it, but no one would respond to my hello. Finally after about a minute of attempting to establish contact with the caller, I hung up the receiver. This action was all repeated in about ten minutes. This peculiar action became a little more clear to me about 10:30 when one of my neighbors called to tell me that he had received a call that evening asking a bunch of questions about me, such as: Was I a good neighbor? Did I have any noticeable character flaws? Did I drink socially? Did I attend church regularly? Had he ever heard me comment on my thoughts toward capital punishment? And, last, had he ever heard me discuss the Ruby case with anyone?

After talking to this neighbor, I called a couple of other neighbors and learned they too had been asked questions about me that same evening. I was convinced that those calls my neighbors received plus the two that I had received were all part of the same investigation. I figured that this was a part of an investigation to learn as much about me as possible prior to my questioning as to juror qualification. This questioning I felt sure was to occur the next day, Thursday. I reasoned that the party who called me only called my number in an attempt to possibly hear over the phone if I had the late evening news on the TV. Of course, if I had been watching the late news and had the volume up, then the caller could have heard the sound and could have reported this to the court during my questioning. However, the TV was not tuned to the newscast. I never did learn if the state or the defense conducted this investigation.

Thursday morning, I was instructed to wait outside Judge Brown's courtroom until my call came to go inside for questioning. The wait was a lengthy one. It lasted from about 9:30 A.M. until 11:25 A.M. I was finally called into the courtroom where I was seated in the witness box. The courtroom was the first one that I had ever been in and it was filled to capacity with spectators and newsmen from all over the world. It was difficult for me to hide my nervousness. District Attorney Henry Wade began to question me. He quizzed me on how I felt about giving the death penalty in cases of proven murder with malice. After approximately twenty minutes of questioning, Mr. Wade passed me to the defense. At this time, 11:45 A.M., Judge Brown recessed the court for lunch until 1:45 P.M. I was admonished about discussing the case and released without restraint until 1:45 P.M.

I had two hours for lunch and no appetite, so I walked the several blocks east from the courthouse to midtown where I entered the Eatwell

Restaurant on Main Street. I ordered a bowl of tomato soup and a glass of iced tea. By the time I had finished the light lunch it was 12:45. I still had an hour to kill.

Dallas weather that Thursday was exceptionally nice for a February afternoon. The temperature at noon was in the upper 50s, a bit nippy in the shade but pleasantly comfortable in the warm sunlight. As I now look back on that leisurely walk back to the courthouse, I recall stopping many times to gaze into the window displays along Main Street, looking but not really seeing that which was being displayed. My mind was preoccupied contemplating just what it would be like when I again stepped inside the courtroom and into the witness box. The defense I felt certain would try to disqualify me as a juror. Many thoughts went through my mind. The most recurring one was that I must not allow myself to become confused or mixed up when I faced the anticipated rapid-fire questions of the chief defense counsel, Mr. Melvin Belli. All I intended to do was to state the truth about what I had seen, heard, and read since 24 November 1963 regarding the Ruby case. However, I felt certain that no matter how careful I was with my answers, that some time during my examination I would become mixed up or confused over some legal technicality that would disqualify me as a juror on the case. This was not poor reasoning on my part since twenty-three prospective jurors had gone the route and not one juror had yet been accepted. I certainly didn't have any desire to serve on this jury but I didn't want to be disqualified because of any stupid answers. I sincerely felt that I could be as fair a juror as it was possible to select. I had little doubt but that the defense counsel would find reason to strike me from qualification as they had the previous twenty-three. (I was number twenty-six, but numbers twenty-one and twenty-five had previously been excused by Judge Brown.)

Having reassured myself that I would not be found acceptable by the defense counsel, I glanced at my watch for what was probably the hundredth time in the past one and one-half hours. It was 1:20 P.M., twenty-five more minutes to wait. I returned to the Criminal Courts Building, and rode the elevator up to the sixth floor where I used the restroom (this was the only restroom I had located). I checked my appearance in the mirror to make certain that my lunch wasn't showing and strolled back down the hall to the elevator that carried me back to the first floor. From the elevator, I walked out the south door and re-entered the building on Main Street at the other south entryway which allowed entrance to the stairway that led up to the courtroom. The stairway was packed, as usual, with newsmen and other curious specta-tors. I elbowed my way to the top of the stairs where I asked a uni-formed deputy sheriff where I should wait the next ten minutes (it was 1:35). He escorted me through the crowd and into the courtroom.

As I was seated in the witness box, I remember thinking that my three and one-half days of waiting were up. If I were lucky in an hour or two at the most, I would certainly be found unacceptable as a juror and dismissed to return home to my family. The defense counsel who questioned me was, as I had feared, Mr. Belli. [Excerpts of Belli's ex-amination of Causey appear in Section III.] However, it was not as bad as I had feared. I was not too ill at ease under his questioning. He was courteous, charming, and eloquently smooth. The questioning was thorough and deliberate. He asked me about my knowledge of the Oswald shooting, what I had read, had I seen it on TV. I told him that I had viewed the TV rerun of the shooting. He made some statement to the court about wanting to summon me as a witness in the case.

Besides unsuccessfully seeking a change of venue in the case, Ruby's defense team bitterly complained that Judge Brown allowed those who had seen the shooting either live or in a replay to serve as jurors. Belli and Tonahill claimed that Texas law prevented a "witness" to a crime from serving on a jury. They went so far as to have each pro-spective juror who had seen the murder on television subpoenaed as a witness, so, theoretically, they would then have to be dismissed (Weinberg and Richmond 1964). Judge Brown upheld the prosecution's objections to the gambit. Finally, Belli appealed the decision allowing television viewers of the killing to serve on the jury to the Texas Supreme Court, even as jury selection proceeded, but the court refused to hear the case (Richmond and Fenley 1964, 1-A).

Then Judge Brown asked me if I could set aside what I had seen on TV and judge the defendant based on the evidence that I would hear.

I answered that I felt that I could honestly do this. Mr. Belli asked me question after question with frequent objections from the prosecuting counsel. As the questioning continued it became increasingly apparent to me that thus far I had not given an answer that I felt justified my rejection, which I still felt was a certainty.

After about one hour of questioning and after Judge Brown had refused to grant the defense counsel additional peremptory challenges, the defense went into a whispered conference with Ruby. I became very uncomfortable, but I fully expected Mr. Belli to break from the conference and use his strike prerogative to delete me as a juror. After a three- or four-minute conference, Mr. Belli rose to his feet and passed the juror qualification acceptance back to the state. [The transcripts show it was actually Joe Tonahill.] Mr. Wade rose to his feet and stated that the state would accept me as a juror. Wade then sat down. Mr. Belli again rose to his feet and to the amazement of everyone in the courtroom, most of all me, he stated that the defense had no objection to me as a juror and that I was acceptable.

In my thirty-five years on this planet I had never been exposed to a more devastating shock than at that moment. I suddenly felt as though the ceiling and all the upper seven floors of the building had collapsed on my head. The next thing I remember was that Judge Brown was speaking to me, to swear me in with the oath of a juror. I recall trying to stand but Judge Brown allowed me to remain seated for the oath. Pandemonium reigned within the courtroom; newsmen catapulted across the room and jammed the doorway in an effort to get their story on the wire, that at last a juror had been accepted.

In his book, *Dallas Justice*, Melvin Belli describes the selection of Max Causey as the first juror this way: "'Why pick him?' the scrawled note in my trial book asks me after the double-underlined name Max E. Causey. And my book answers, 'a) knew psychology in education, b) weak (?) on cap punishment, c) smiles at me.' In retrospect, Causey's smile holds little cheer for me, but he appeared a not unlikely choice when, after three and one-half days and twenty-three panelists, we finally agreed to accept him as juror number one.

"A chunky man with close-cropped reddish hair, Causey stepped to the stand at 11:38 A.M. on the trial's fourth day and identified himself as a cost analyst at Ling-Temco-Vought, one of the major electronics firms in the Dallas area, as a thirty-five-year-old father of two, as a member of the First Baptist Church in suburban Garland. He sat hunched forward with a pained expression on his face, two deep, troubled furrows between his eyes. The prosecution questioned him briefly. His last words before we stopped for lunch were, 'I really believe I have no opinion.'

"I started questioning him at 1:46. He had had a good view of the shooting on a TV rerun, he said. Yes, it would be difficult to erase that image from his mind. Yes, he still had a lingering opinion. Judge Brown interrupted: Could Mr. Causey set his opinions aside and be a fair, impartial juror? Mr. Causey thought he could set them aside. He had a master's degree in education, he said, and had studied some psychology. No, he had no prejudice against a man who ran a strip-tease joint. Yes, he would insist that guilt be proven beyond a reasonable doubt. . . . Under normal circumstances, I would have rejected Causey, but we had only those fifteen peremptory challenges.

"When the reporters asked me at session's end, I said, 'We've got an alert, intelligent juror.' The next morning, I read in the newspapers that his wife, interviewed, had said, 'I remember Max talking about his feelings on capital punishment. He told me he would like to see it abolished, but as long as it's the law, he believes in abiding by it.' (An encouraging note to savor along with the Friday morning coffee.) Later on, the interviewer quoted her as saying, 'I think I will send Belli a little message and tell him to hurry and let my husband come home. . . .' (The coffee seemed tepid by now. 'Send Belli a little message.' It made you wonder if she placed all the blame for the lengthiness of the trial on me.)" (Belli 1964, 131–132)

After I had taken the oath, the court bailiff, Mr. Bo Mabra, quickly escorted me through a locked door immediately behind the judge's bench. We went up a flight of stairs to a large suite which was used as the jury deliberation room and day quarters for the jury when they were not in the jury box. This was to be my day quarters during the

many days ahead, while downstairs the long, slow deliberate jury qualification continued in the quest for the other eleven jurors. As I climbed
those stairs that first time I remember asking the bailiff a question to
which I really already knew the answer, but I had to hear it from him:
"Was I the first?" Of course, his answer was in the affirmative. The
bailiff made me as comfortable as a man in my present state of mind
could be, and he hurriedly returned to the courtroom, locking the
massive door at the foot of the stairs. The locked door served a dual
role: One was to keep anyone from approaching me, and the other was
to restrain me if need be.

Not until the bailiff left me alone for the first time did the full momentous impact of what was happening began to settle over me as a
choking, smothering shroud. I looked around my quarters and found
that there was one long table in the main room with twelve chairs, and
off in an alcove to the east was another room about fifteen-by-fifteen
feet that had lounge chairs and reading lamps. The quarters under any
other set of circumstances would have been quite comfortable. But I
was too concerned pondering my personal fate to appreciate the comfort that might be here. I began to wonder how this would affect my
wife and family. I had always handled most of the financial and business
affairs, and I didn't know just how they would fare without me. My wife
and I had always discussed our financial needs and desires, but the ultimate responsibility of the final decision had always been mine. How
could my wife handle these new responsibilities? Could she cope with all
the little family crises that arise from day to day? In short, could she be
both a mother and a father to the family for an extended period?

**Causey makes no direct reference to it, but his and his wife's
younger child, Kevin, was severely afflicted with a genetic disease,
phenylketonuria (PKU), that prevents the normal use of protein foods.
Although five years old at the time of the Ruby trial, Kevin had to be
cared for as an infant, twenty-four hours a day. This no doubt weighed
heavily on his mind. Kevin died of the disease in 1966.**

What about my employer Ling-Temco-Vought? This was also a
grave concern to me, although the firm encouraged all its employees

Rosemary and Keith Causey, February 1964. From the collection of Max and Rosemary Causey.

to serve their civic responsibilities such as serving on jury duty. Normally the company very generously paid the salaries of its employees who served on jury duty, but just how long would they continue to do so? Who could foresee an employee being assigned to confining jury duty which could, I believed, last for days, weeks, or perhaps longer. Who could tell? Would my pay continue throughout a long and prolonged trial? If not, my financial situation would become crucial very shortly. Unfortunately, our checking account could not withstand the omission of even one bimonthly paycheck. The financial drain of a home mortgage, new car, doctor bills, insurance, and other family expenses required a delicate balancing of the budget. Also, my duties with the company had just recently changed in that I had just been assigned new responsibilities on a new contract. I was to have the responsibility of planning, scheduling, and cost control on this new contract. In my absence the job might be handed over to someone else to handle, and where would this leave me?

I continued to explore many troubled thoughts during that first afternoon as I paced the floor and frequently glanced at my watch. Somehow, there just wasn't much comfort that I could find in the situation I had gotten myself into. I kept thinking why didn't I just tell the court that I could not give the death penalty under any set of circumstances and I would surely have been dismissed by the judge. But on the other hand, this just wasn't the truth, and I had to live with myself after this case became ancient history. As I paced the floor, glancing every few minutes at my watch, the afternoon dragged laboriously on until 5:30 when the bailiff returned. At the head of the stairs just outside my suite he greeted me with, "Hey, Max, have you jumped out a window yet?" It really wasn't funny but I forced a laugh as I returned the greeting. It was great to have someone's company again after two and one-half hours of pondering my personal situation.

The next hour was spent getting familiar with my sleeping quarters. The quarters were far short of the comforts of home but fully adequate for their purpose. The bedroom was about seven-by-seven feet, with a built-in, comfortable bunk bed, lavatory, and commode, with a shaving mirror over the lavatory. A tiled shower was next door to my room, and on the same side of the hall were six other rooms beside mine. Across the hall from my room was the bailiff's room, with six more rooms on that side of the hall. All the rooms were identical with the exception of the one that the bailiff occupied, and this room had a wall telephone. This telephone was to be our emergency link with the outside world for the next few weeks. Although at no time was I allowed to talk to anyone over this phone, it was some comfort to know that it was there in the event that an emergency should arise within my family.

As soon as we had completed the tour of our night quarters, the bailiff called my wife to inform her that I was to be detained as a guest of the state for awhile. The bailiff asked my wife to pack a suitcase with several changes of clothes and necessary toilet articles to last several days. She was told to put in some casual clothes for our leisure hours. She was told to deliver the clothes to the sheriff's office and the bailiff would pick them up for me.

The bailiff also warned my wife that she might expect to be

approached by the news media for interviews. To this she laughed, telling him that at the present time two national TV networks were already setting up in our living room in preparation for interviews with her and the children. She told Bo that since 3:00 P.M., there had been a steady flow of newsmen in and out of our house to the point that it was beginning to look like a political convention was being held there. Bo told her that if she got tired of the newsmen to order them out and if they resisted for her to call his number and he would take care of the problem. I found out later that our house was patrolled by sheriff's cars or Garland police cars at frequent intervals and any one of them could have gone to her assistance with just a call from Bo. He gave her his phone number and told her that she could always reach him there at night in the event of an emergency.

At about 7:00 P.M., the bailiff suggested we go out to dinner. I welcomed the thought of getting out in the open but I really didn't feel too hungry. We stepped out of the Criminal Courts Building into the cold, damp night. A fast-moving cold front had engulfed Dallas since I had been out to lunch some six hours earlier. We walked the three blocks to the Dallas-Jefferson Hotel on Houston Street where we ordered dinner. The food, under any other circumstances, I'm sure would have been delicious but I could only pick at it. I had no appetite for food at that time. We returned to our sleeping quarters around 8:00 P.M. By this time my wife had sent the luggage that I would require for a prolonged stay. She had sent it to the sheriff's office, where we picked it up.

Bo and I talked awhile and soon I found that he was a very friendly, considerate, and likable person, ideally suited for his job. He was to be my nursemaid, den mother, chaplain, doctor, and most important, my only link to the world outside for the next few weeks. Bo told me that he had held the same job for more than eight years, during which time he had played nursemaid to many such jury panels. It was old stuff to him. We drank coffee and discussed the prospects of how long our confinement might last. Our most optimistic estimate was three weeks. Neither of us dared to predict how much longer it would take once the jury was finally picked to hear all the evidence in court and reach a decision as to the innocence or guilt of Mr. Ruby.

I went to bed that first night contemplating what lay ahead. I wondered who might be the second juror and how long would it take to pick him, or her. Would it take as long to pick the second as it had taken to pick the first? I concluded that if this were to be the case, then I would surely be alone for three or four more days. With a Sunday coming up this would mean that I most likely would not have a juror companion until Monday or Tuesday. As I lay alone in bed, my mind raced over and over again all the thoughts that I first entertained when I realized I had been accepted. But in the dark hours of night, additional problems began to crop up. My mind kept cycling and recycling until I mercifully lapsed into unconsciousness. I slept fitfully until 3:00 A.M., at which time I looked at my watch and thought, Would this night never end? For the next three hours I catnapped, waking after a few minutes thinking that it was all one big bad dream, that this had not really happened to me. At last I heard Bo in the shower next door to my room. Thank heaven it was morning.

My second day started with a shave and quick shower. By the time I had dressed, Bo had brought coffee down from the jail kitchen. We leisurely sipped our coffee and talked about the probable number of jurors that might likely be questioned today. We discussed the possibility that the original 150 prospective jurors assigned to the panel might not be enough from which to select twelve jurors, assuming the rejection rate were to continue as it had in the past. Already nearly thirty had been questioned with me being the only one selected. It didn't take a mathematician to figure out that at this rate the 150 could only provide about five or six jurors. We finished our coffee and then went downstairs and out to breakfast.

As we stepped out of the building onto the street, we were greeted with a bitterly cold wind. During the night, a light snow had fallen and snow was sprinkled over the autos parked on the street, and an occasional snowflake still fluttered from a dark, overcast sky. At the entrance to the courthouse, the press and spectators had already commenced to assemble with still two hours before the jury selection was to recommence. It was hard for me to comprehend why spectators would stand out in the bitter cold fighting for a chance to get into the courtroom. Bo had told me that the seating capacity of the courtroom was about 200, with most of these seats delegated to the press and news media. As we walked along the street toward our breakfast, we passed a newspaper stand, and I could not help but observe that I had made the front page. Bo could not allow me to read the newspaper, but he did allow me to see pictures of my wife and older son on the front page. I certainly had not anticipated all the publicity that came with being selected as the first juror. I wondered how my wife must have felt when she was suddenly the target of the questions from the news media.

After breakfast, which consisted of a sweet roll and coffee, we returned to the courts building and struggled through the throng up the stairway and into the courtroom. The courtroom had not yet been opened to the news media and except for a few members of the courthouse staff it was still empty. Bo led me through the empty courtroom and back up the stairs to my day quarters. Here my long and lonely vigil was to resume. While pacing the floor, it suddenly occurred to me that I could at least write down some notes as to how I felt about all of the activity up to now. I sat down at the long jury table and commenced to reconstruct on paper all the significant events that I could recall over the past two days. This turned out to be an excellent way of spending my time.

At approximately 11:45, Bo returned and suggested that it would be better if we stayed in the room for lunch, since he had received word that the news media were waiting on the street exit for photographs and questioning. Of course, Judge Brown had strictly forbidden any action of this nature. In order to avoid this probable confrontation, I agreed that sandwiches brought up to the room would be all right with me. Bo went out and came back with sandwiches and soda pop.

As we ate, I pumped Bo for as much information as he was allowed to relay to me. I was particularly interested in the number of prospective jurors that had been rejected during the course of the morning's questioning. My interest here was due to the fact that I knew Judge Brown had granted both the defense and the prosecution fifteen strikes each. This is to say that both the defense and the state attorneys could reject fifteen prospective jurors on peremptory challenges without stating any reason for the rejection. Any prospective juror who did not qualify in the judge's opinion could be stricken without it being charged either to the defense or the state. My reasoning was simple mathematics. Since I knew that the defense had already used five strikes when I was accepted, this left them with ten remaining strikes and over 100 prospective jurors to question. The more strikes used by the defense or the state reduced the remaining available strikes left to them, and presumably might speed up the jury selection process. Of course, this reasoning assumed that Judge Brown would not grant additional strikes to either party. It seemed logical to me that as either the defense or the state began to run critically short on strikes they would become a little less critical of the jurors. Bo told me that during the morning the defense had used up two more of its strikes and Judge Brown had disqualified two. This brought the box score to thirty-four prospects questioned and one selected with the defense having eight remaining strikes and the state with thirteen.

With the lunch recess over, Bo returned to his duties in the courtroom. Left alone again, I tried to kill time by playing solitaire. After numerous failures to beat "Sol," I had just about given up when I heard the lock turn on the massive door at the foot of the stairs. The noise and excitement coming from the courtroom below alerted me to the fact that something must have changed in the normal routine. Then I heard footsteps. This time there were footsteps of two people. Bo was not alone. Excitement swelled within me as I waited for them to appear at the top of the stairs. I was really in luck. Not only was Bo bringing me a companion, but I recognized him as one of the prospective jurors whom I had lunched with a couple of days before. The second juror was Mr. Allen McCoy from the suburb of Irving. I greeted McCoy with a warm handshake and offered him a cup of coffee. My "solitaire" wait was over. I looked at my watch and noted that it was 3:55 P.M. After 25 hours, I had a companion to share the lonely wait with.

I explained to Allen what I knew about our quarters and the daily routine we would pursue while we waited for juror number three. It was apparent that Allen was not as shocked about his selection as I had been with mine. He seemed to accept the role that had been dealt him and showed no outward concern for the confinement that lay ahead. Allen and I talked and the next hour and one-half passed more swiftly than any that I had endured since I was selected. Bo returned to us at 5:30, alone this time, and we three proceeded to our night quarters and the "off duty" side of our routine. At 7:00 P.M., Bo carried us out to dinner. This was the first time in about thirty-six hours that I really felt hungry. After dinner we walked around the street for about twenty minutes before returning to our night quarters. We talked and read magazines until around 11:00 P.M., when we each retired to our separate rooms and to bed.

The following day was Saturday, 22 February 1964, and was to be a regular working day for the court. We awoke at 6:00 A.M., anxious for the day to start. We were somewhat optimistic about a quicker selection of the jurors than I had been just twenty-four hours before. We had the usual breakfast at Malendorf's, a small cafeteria-type restaurant located across the street, east of the Criminal Courts Building. After a breakfast of coffee and sweet rolls, we returned to the familiar twenty steps up the stairs that led to our day quarters. Bo left us and returned to his duties in the courtroom below, and together we patiently waited for juror number three. Our earlier optimism suffered a severe setback at 12:30 when Bo returned and informed us that Judge Brown had recessed court until 9:00 A.M. Monday. No additional jurors had been accepted, so Allen, Bo, and I faced a weekend of confinement, during which time there was no progress being made toward the juror selection. This was to be my first weekend away from my family in over eight years. I wasn't looking forward to this separation. However, it didn't turn out as bad as I had expected thanks to the thoughtfulness of Bo. He had received permission from Sheriff Decker to take us anywhere within the city limits to restaurants of our choice during the long weekend recess. This welcome break with our daily routine helped to pass the time, and we enjoyed eating a late Saturday lunch and early Sunday dinner in the suburban restaurants. Sunday afternoon we drove out to the southwestern edge of the county and watched skydivers leap from aircraft and spot jump. We watched this about for about two hours and drove back in.

Monday morning signaled the start of the second week of juror selection. Allen and I were eager for the court to resume its questioning of prospective jurors. We were rewarded at 11:15 when we heard the big door at the foot of the stairs open and the now familiar sound of the courtroom noise and the sound of footsteps coming up the stairs—two sets of footsteps. Bo brought in to us and introduced juror number three, Mrs. Mildred McCollum. Mildred was the first female juror and thus resulted in the assignment of a lady bailiff to join our number. The lady bailiff proved to be just as well-suited for her job as was Bo. She was Mrs. Nell Tyler, and she was assigned to care for Mildred's needs the same as Bo was doing for Allen and me. Now our number was five when we went out to eat our meals.

During our lunch walk, we were bothered a bit by news photographers trying to get photographs of the jury. Judge Brown had warned the photographers that photos would not be allowed. However, nothing could prevent these dedicated men from taking distant shots with telescopic lenses. We were not too surprised when we saw our picture on the front page of the Tuesday morning *Dallas Morning News.* Monday had ended with only the three of us selected. Monday night the five of us—Allen, Mildred, Bo, Nell, and I—went to dinner as a group.

Tuesday, 25 February, we believed would be a profitable day in the jury selection. We took our usual place in our day quarters and settled down to wait for juror number four. Mercifully, we didn't have to wait but about two hours because shortly before 11:00 A.M., we heard that familiar sound coming from the courtroom and the sound of two sets of footsteps coming up the stairs. We were introduced to juror number four. He was Mr. Gene Dickerson of the suburb of Mesquite. We filled him in with the routine as we had come to know it. Before we had completed our indoctrination of Gene, we were much surprised to be greeted with juror number five, Mr. Doug Sowell of Dallas Oak Cliff. At noon, our number including the two bailiffs was seven.

During our lunch, which we ate at the Dallas-Jefferson Hotel, the photographers, completely disregarding Judge Brown's earlier instructions, proceeded to descend upon us from every angle with camera shutters snapping. Bo would repeatedly drive them back a few tables but it was obvious that they were not going to be denied their photographs. We continued to act as naturally as possible, pretending not to notice that they were there. As we left the dining room, they were waiting at the entrance for more photographs. As we walked along the route back to the courthouse, the photographers would run ahead of us and snap photographs as we walked past. It was amusing how they were getting in each other's camera view. There must have been as many as eight or ten of these men madly dashing out in front of our intended path to get better angles. All of this publicity was a little exciting but it was far more frightening. Everyone concerned with the security of the jury felt that no good could possibly come from this much exposure to the public. Later on, many of us were to better understand this.

The two jurors selected during the morning were all for the day, but we had enough members that we could pass the hours away playing cards or dominoes. Tuesday night the five of us and the two bailiffs piled into Bo's car and drove out to the Flight Deck Restaurant at Dallas Love Field airport for dinner. The change of scenery did wonders for our morale.

Wednesday, 26 February, was one of our best days for seeing our number grow. At approximately 10:20 we were joined by juror number six. He was R. J. "Bob" Flechtner of Richardson. Flechtner was followed before lunch by juror number seven, Mrs. Gwen English of Dallas.

If we thought that we had been exposed to the photographers on Tuesday, then we really didn't know what real exposure was like until lunch on this day. All along our route to lunch there were photographers climbing up utility poles and on top of automobiles to get better shots of us. One photographer climbed upon a large corner mailbox directly in front of us and was snapping away with his camera.

After lunch we had about a two-hour wait before we were introduced to juror number eight, Mr. Glenn Holton. This was the best day thus far for the selection of jurors, with three being selected. We also learned from Mr. Holton that the defense this day had used another peremptory challenge, leaving them with only four left. The state had used five challenges and the defense eleven to date. Somehow, we all felt that time was rapidly approaching when we would be complete in number. That evening we walked about five blocks east toward downtown to have dinner at Vincent's Seafood Restaurant. Looking around the dinner table that evening, I could not help but contemplate just how long before the other four positions would be filled on our jury.

Thursday, 27 February, commenced with the usual breakfast of coffee and sweet rolls at Malendorf's. Back in our day quarters, we patiently awaited juror number nine. We had a long wait. Lunch came and went and still no addition, then about 5:00 P.M. we cheered the arrival of Mr. Jim Cunningham, juror number nine. Thursday ended with the nine selected jurors. The defense had now used thirteen of its fifteen challenges. We anticipated that the defense would now be forced into being a little less choosy in picking the jurors.

Friday, 28 February, brought us the same routine as the past days. However, we did think up a new game for passing the time away. Someone came up with the idea to divide up the Monopoly play money among about five of us guys who wanted to play some poker, just for fun. This turned out to be most interesting to see who would end up with all the money and who would go broke the quickest. With our number now up to nine, we had enough for different games to be played at the same time. We had some bridge players, "42" players, and those who preferred dominoes, checkers, and Monopoly besides our friendly poker players. All of these activities helped to shorten the day and by the end of this day we had reached ten. We most eagerly greeted Mr. J. Waymon Rose in his role as juror number ten.

Belli later wrote: "There was betting on the press benches that Max Causey would be the leader [of the jury]; he had that substantial air that people expect in a committee chairman, and he certainly had the claim of seniority—it was more than a week now that poor Causey had been confined to that dreary, sunless jury room except for brief guided excursions for meals. Causey eventually was chosen foreman, but my choice for leader is now as it was then, J. Waymon Rose. . . . It came out that he had retired from the Naval Reserve the previous year after long service which had included sitting on two courts martial." Belli was impressed when Rose told the story of a University of Alabama football player who came off the bench in the Cotton Bowl to tackle a Rice University ball carrier who was breaking free down the sideline. Rose told the story to illustrate that he understood how someone could get "carried away" (Belli 1964, 138–139).

Saturday, 29 February was the last day of the month and for me this was my tenth day of confinement. Most of us were apprehensive about filling the jury today. About noon, Bo came up the stairs and informed us that Judge Brown had recessed the court until 9:00 A.M. Monday. No juror had been selected and now we knew that two more days would have to pass before another could possibly be accepted. We sadly looked forward to the weekend of continuing confinement, my second.

However, this weekend we were unexpectedly rewarded when Bo told us that Judge Brown had met with the defense lawyers and the lawyers for the state and all had agreed that for the first time we would be allowed to have a TV in the lounge room of our night quarters. There were, of course, certain restrictions, such as no newscast audio and no medical or legal shows. *Perry Mason* was definitely out. Despite the restrictions, it was great to once again be able to view TV programs. On Saturday, Bo carried several of the men to a nearby barbershop for much-needed haircuts. Nell stayed with the other group until Bo returned with us. Sunday morning, after sleeping late, we walked several blocks east to the Baker Hotel Coffee Shop, where we all enjoyed a very leisurely breakfast in an atmosphere that would almost allow one to forget the real situation. Despite the TV and the good breakfast, I didn't forget for very long how much I was missing my dear wife and children.

Monday, 2 March, started the third week of jury selection and it was my twelfth day of confinement. I never realized before so completely the meaning of freedom. However, it was not the twelve days that had passed that caused me grief as much as the worry about how many more days might lie ahead. Once the jury was complete, how long might the trial itself take? This was a question that no one could answer. When this day passed without another juror being selected, I felt the lowest that I had felt since the first day of my selection. We had now gone through two days of questioning since the last one had been accepted. Sometimes I felt that maybe we had been too conservative with our most pessimistic guesses as to how long this entire case might last.

This group of jurors was outstanding. The intelligence level was well above that of the average jury. There wasn't a single personality on the jury thus far who didn't bring credit to the entire group. There had not been even a cross word between us, and under the confining conditions, that had to be good. There was a remarkable cross section of occupations. Engineers, administrators, salesmen, a postman, a mechanic, a secretary, and an executive were some of the positions these jurors held. The jovial personalities of a couple were such that their constant witty remarks kept the entire group guessing about what they might say or do next. We could be jovial now because we all knew that once the last juror was accepted, the job we were expected to perform would not be a happy, jovial task, nor did we expect that it would be an easy one.

One of the "jovial personalities" was surely Waymon Rose. In a newspaper article after the trial, bailiff Bo Mabra was quoted as saying Rose gave jurors a lift during idle periods. When told jurors could have only a single beer when they went out to dinner, Rose was quoted as saying, "Let's go where they serve quarts" (Biffle 1964, 16-A).

Each juror was aware of the seriousness of the task that lay ahead of us. I had considerable dread for the job we would be asked to do. I had never sat on a jury, and I really didn't know just what to expect. From what we had heard before we had ever been summoned to the jury panel, we knew that the defense lawyers were the very best that this country had to offer and the Dallas County District Attorney's Office also had an excellent record. Every indication would only suggest that in the final analysis, we the jury would have to make a very difficult decision based on the facts that would be presented to us during the trial. I also wondered about the possibility of getting all twelve of the jurors to agree that the evidence indicated a unanimous decision.

Tuesday, 3 March, brought a general letdown in our group regarding selection of jurors numbers eleven and twelve. We now felt that it may be near the end of the week before we would have the final juror. The state had now used eleven strikes and the defense had used all of the original fifteen, plus three more that had been granted to them.

Belli had asked for three additional peremptory challenges and Judge Brown granted his request. Authors Kaplan and Waltz ob-

served (1965, 108): "By giving the defense three extra [peremptory challenges], Judge Brown was insulating himself from possible reversal for mistakenly qualifying three jurors. Of course, the major issue—the question of whether those who had viewed Oswald's killing on television were ineligible to sit as jurors—was in no way resolved by the judge's generosity."

I thought the defense was now in the position of having to offend or anger a prospective juror whom they felt was not acceptable for their client's case. If they could force a prospect to become angry, then Judge Brown could strike him on a disqualification. Needless to say, this type of questioning would have been very time-consuming and certainly not conducive to the expedient selection of jurors eleven and twelve. Despite the slowness of the selection, we fervently hoped it wouldn't be too much longer before the final two would be selected.

Juror number eleven joined our group at about 10:30 A.M. March 3. She was Mrs. Aileen Shields of Dallas. Talking with Aileen, we learned that Judge Brown was out sick and that Judge J. Frank Wilson was presiding in his absence. I was startled to learn that it was legal for one judge to replace another once the jury selection had commenced. I knew that no one of our number could be replaced, and that if one of us became ill or had an emergency that forced our removal from the jury, then the rest of us would then be excused. I asked Bo about the legality of Judge Wilson replacing Judge Brown, and he told me that it was legal since precedent had been established. There had been momentary apprehension on my part about the possibility that such a change might be grounds for a retrial and that the jury might be dismissed.

In fact, on the day the presentation of evidence in the trial began, Wednesday, March 4, Belli asked for two additional peremptory challenges, with which he intended to remove the final two jurors who had been selected, Mrs. Shields and Mrs. Louise Malone. His justification was that the jurors were selected on a day when Judge Brown was absent and was replaced by another judge, Frank Wilson. Wilson, Belli said, "did not have jurisdiction to sit during the picking of those two jurors." Judge Brown denied this request and the trial proceeded (Statement of Facts, 2).

Judge J. Frank Wilson was considered a much stricter judge than Judge Brown. "Judge Wilson . . . was distinctly stern of temperament and it became clear that he had been displeased by reports of the general disorder in his courtroom [the trial was being held in what was normally Wilson's court]. . . . Every lawyer in the room realized that he [Wilson] was far more likely than Brown to take swift and serious action should any breach of decorum occur." It was on this day that the jury selection was finally completed (Kaplan and Waltz 1965, 113).

When the Texas Court of Criminal Appeals reversed and remanded the verdict of the Ruby trial in October 1966, the controversy over the selection of Mrs. Shields and Mrs. Malone was specifically mentioned. But the fact that Mrs. Shields and Mrs. Malone, like almost all of the other jurors, had seen the killing of Mr. Oswald on television was a stronger reason in the decision to order a new trial. As Judge McDonald wrote: "Ten of Jack Ruby's trial jurors witnessed the shooting of Oswald on television. They were challenged for cause under Article 16, Vernon's Ann. C.C.P., which prohibits a witness serving as a juror. Such challenges for cause were summarily dismissed. . . . There can be no difference to the competency of a witness who has heard via telephone or radio, or saw a matter through a mirror or field glasses, and a witness who has viewed a matter on television. . . . In short, the television viewer meets the established criterion of personal observation required for a witness's competency."

McDonald also commented: "The writer feels it is fair to assume that the citizenry of Dallas consciously and subconsciously felt Dallas was on trial and the Dallas image was uppermost in their minds to such an extent that Ruby could not be tried there fairly while the state, nation, and world judged Dallas for the tragic November events."

The appeals court ruled that Judge Brown's decision not to grant Mr. Ruby's motion for a change of venue was a reversible error (*J. Rubenstein, alias Jack Ruby, appellant v. The State of Texas, appellee*, No. 37900, 407 S.W. 2d 793, Court of Criminal Appeals of Texas,

Oct. 5, 1966). Mr. Ruby died, still in the custody of the Dallas County Sheriff, in January 1967, before a new trial could be held.

The most important juror of all, juror number twelve, joined our group at about 2:30 P.M., March 3. Mrs. Louise Malone was greeted with a standing ovation from the other eleven jurors. It was the happiest moment that I had known in nearly two weeks. We at last were complete and looked forward to occupying the jury box downstairs. For the past thirteen days, I had been locked up just a few feet away from where all the action was taking place. Now, at long last, I could start fulfilling the job for which I had been selected. I believe that each member of the jury felt that he or she was a member of a dedicated team, an all-star team having been so meticulously chosen by both the defense and the state lawyers. Somehow, we felt that we had been called upon to perform a function for which more than 150 others had not been chosen. There was a heavy responsibility resting on our shoulders, a responsibility to render the proper and justifiable verdict based on the evidence that we would hear in the courtroom.

Shortly after the twelfth juror joined us, Bo came back and told us that the trial was scheduled to commence at 9:00 A.M. Wednesday morning. Bo and Nell ushered us back to our night quarters earlier than usual that afternoon. We decided that in view of the occasion, we should go out to a good restaurant for dinner. Bo told us to decide where we would like to go and he would arrange for transportation for us. We all had to agree on the same place because there could be no splitting up of the jury. Several places were mentioned and finally the Jack Ruby jury took its first vote. I was surprised when we all agreed unanimously to go to Kirby's Steak House. At the time, I wondered if we could agree on the same verdict at the end of the trial as easily as we had for this dinner.

While we cleaned up, Bo made arrangements to have three unmarked sheriff's cars driven by deputies transport us to dinner. Every evening that was to follow reflected the same routine in our method of transportation to our evening meal. Each night our selected destination was kept a secret even from the drivers until all three cars were loaded. Then Bo would tell each driver where we were going and then the cars would drive out one behind the other, keeping in sight of one another at all times. Prior to our departure, Bo would call ahead to the selected restaurant and make secret arrangements for the jury to be seated in a wing section or secluded corner that could be secured from photographers, newsmen, and other persons seeking contact with the jury. Sometimes it was a game that the deputy sheriffs would play trying to elude the crowd of photographers that was constantly trying to sneak photos of the complete jury.

Wednesday, 4 March, we had breakfast and returned to our day quarters where we made a big pot of coffee and settled down to await our call to sit in the jury box for the first time. We really didn't expect to start hearing testimony until late in the morning due to anticipated routine motions that Judge Brown would have to hear. However, we did get to hear about one hour and fifty minutes of testimony in the morning.

The first witness called by the prosecution was Don Campbell, an advertising salesman with *The Dallas Morning News*. Campbell worked with Ruby in preparing newspaper ads for his nightclub. Campbell testified that Ruby was "competent" in writing his own ads. Later, Garnet Claude Hallmark, the general manager of All Right Auto Parking where Ruby had parked his car for three years, described Ruby as a "preoccupied and intense person." Under cross-examination by defense counsel Tonahill, Hallmark said he "sometimes wondered about Jack's sanity" (Statement of Facts, 27–28, 127, 128).

Judge Brown had recovered and was now back on the bench. The trial got under way when the jury was marched in to take our seats. The rest of the courtroom was already full. Once we were seated, Mr. Henry Wade, the district attorney, walked over to face Jack Ruby and read the charge to him. Mr. Ruby's reply to the charge was "not guilty, Your Honor." I think Ruby's defense attorneys were trying to get him to say, "not guilty by reason of insanity," but this was not too clearly audible to us as Judge Brown interrupted this action. The prosecution started off the trial with a parade of state witnesses. Each in turn was cross-examined by the defense in an effort to discredit their testimony or to extract something different from their testimony.

This day's testimony was not hard to follow as it consisted mainly of reconstructing the setting of the crime by witnesses for the state. We heard testimony placing Ruby at the scene only about four minutes prior to the shooting of Oswald. Several Dallas Police detectives testified as to what they saw and heard at the time. The murder weapon was introduced into evidence. One good point for the state was the testimony of Detective J. R. Leavelle, who had been handcuffed to Oswald at the time of the shooting. The detective testified that Ruby had said, while being led past the dying Oswald, "I hope the son of a bitch dies."

Mr. Leavelle is immortalized in the famous photograph of Ruby shooting Lee Harvey Oswald as the tall man in the Stetson and light-colored suit with an anguished expression on his face. Leavelle testified that after Mr. Oswald was shot, he and some other officers carried the dying man back into the jail office in the basement of City Hall. Simultaneously, several other officers wrestled with Ruby and arrested him. One, Mr. L. C. Graves, prevented Mr. Ruby from firing another shot by grabbing the cylinder of the revolver. As Mr. Ruby and the officers were waiting outside the jail office for an elevator that would take him upstairs to be questioned, Mr. Leavelle testified he heard Mr. Ruby say, "I hope the son of a bitch dies." This occurred within about one minute of the shooting, Mr. Leavelle testified.

Defense attorney Melvin Belli objected to this testimony on the grounds that under Texas law, a statement made by a defendant while he is in the custody of a police officer is inadmissible as evidence unless made before a judge or made in writing and signed by the defendant. The judge overruled the objection and said the testimony was admissible as part of the *res gestae* (the spontaneous flow of events or "things done") of the offense (Statement of Facts, 178–179).

Texas courts had traditionally held that oral statements made immediately after committing a crime are admissible, even though the accused may be under arrest at the time (Kaplan and Waltz 1965, 136–37).

In cross-examination, defense attorney Belli attempted to establish that Mr. Ruby, in the throes of a psychomotor epileptic seizure and not realizing what he had done, was responding to shouts in the basement of "Oswald is shot!" by saying, "I hope the son of a bitch dies." Mr. Leavelle unenthusiastically acknowledged it was possible, but it is apparent that Mr. Belli's explanation of Mr. Ruby's comment did not convince the jury (Statement of Facts, 187–88).

A point favoring the defense was the short interval of time that Ruby had between leaving the Western Union office and firing his gun, leaving him little time for premeditation. The first day of testimony ended with our hearing about five hours of testimony.

Western Union supervisor Doyle Lane testified that he had known Ruby casually for about a year when Ruby came into the Western Union office Sunday morning, November 24, to wire money to one of his dancers, who had called him that morning asking for a loan to help pay her rent. Lane testified that he saw "nothing different about him." The time stamped on Ruby's receipt showed 11:17 A.M. Lane testified that Ruby then walked at an "ordinary pace" toward City Hall, where Oswald was being held in the city jail and was about to be transferred to the county jail. Later testimony established that the Western Union office was 339½ feet from the entrance to the ramp where Ruby walked unchallenged into the City Hall basement. Oswald was shot at 11:21 A.M. (Statement of Facts, 141, 142, 145, 166, 195).

Thursday, 5 March, was our second day of hearing testimony. The state continued to parade a number of witnesses to the stand. Detective D. R. Archer corroborated the previous day's statement by Detective Leavelle about Ruby saying "son of a bitch," referring to the dying Oswald. Archer added that Ruby had said he intended to shoot Oswald three times. Detective Thomas Don McMillon following Archer's testimony testified to hearing Ruby say, "You rat son of a bitch, you shot the president."

District Attorney Wade asked Archer, who was standing just outside the basement jail office door as Oswald was led out, if he heard Ruby say any words as he advanced to shoot Oswald. "I heard him say a phrase, I couldn't make out all of it. I did hear the words, 'son of a bitch' . . . It was louder than the rest of the phrase." Archer went on to testify that, after Ruby had been subdued by police, he said, "I hope I killed the son of a bitch." He testified this comment came ten to twelve seconds after the shooting. Belli objected to this testimony on the grounds that it came after Ruby was under arrest and without counsel, but he was overruled. Again over the strenuous objections of Belli, Archer told the court that, after Ruby had been taken upstairs for questioning, Archer said to Ruby, "I think you killed him." To which Ruby replied, "I intended to shoot him three times." Archer said this comment came three to five minutes after the shooting.

As Causey writes, McMillon testified that Ruby said, "You rat son of a bitch . . ." as he stepped forward to kill Oswald. As Belli vehemently objected, Wade asked McMillon if Ruby said anything as he was being hustled out of the basement after the shooting. "He said, 'I hope I killed the son of a bitch. I hope I killed the son of a bitch.' He said it more than once," McMillon responded. Wade asked, "Did you hear him say anything with reference to who he was?" McMillon replied, "He kept hollering, 'You know me, you know me, I'm Jack Ruby'" (Statement of Facts, 248, 250, 252, 253, 255, 297, 300, 302).

Friday, 6 March, was a treat for me in that I got to look at my wife across the courtroom. As we came down the stairs to take our seats in the jury box, Bo whispered to me that my wife was seated in the spectators' section of the courtroom near the center rear. Once seated in the box, I cast a wishful eye in her direction and without any signal at all our eyes met across the crowded courtroom. She looked great to me. This was the first time that I had seen her in fifteen days. In between film showings and witnesses, I would glance at her and always our eyes would meet, and I could see a faint smile sweep across her face. Of course, we never got to speak or signal at all since we were at opposite ends of the courtroom.

Friday morning was spent viewing two television films of the Oswald shooting. We viewed each of the films at regular speed and then in slow motion to pick up specific details. Police Sergeant Patrick T. Dean provided the state with strong testimony pertaining to Ruby's having said that he wanted to kill Oswald after he saw his sneering face on Friday night. Sergeant Dean further testified that Ruby had said he "wanted to kill Oswald to prove to the world that Jews had guts." Both of these statements from Dean were, according to the state, evidence of Ruby's premeditation to kill Oswald. Much to our surprise, Sergeant Dean was the final state witness and the state rested its case against Jack Ruby.

The jurors might have been expecting the prosecution to address the issue of Ruby's sanity. But the prosecutors chose to make no reference to Ruby's soundness of mind, leaving the task of proving his insanity up to the defense, and preparing to refute the testimony of their witnesses (Kaplan and Waltz 1965, 170–171).

Regarding Dean's testimony, Wade asked the officer what Ruby said to him shortly after the shooting. Dean testified that Ruby told him that he had seen Oswald on Friday night, Nov. 22, when Oswald was brought before the media. Dean said Ruby told him he had "noticed the sarcastic sneer on Oswald's face. . . . He said that is when he first thought that if he got the chance, he would kill him. And also that he guessed that he wanted the world to know that Jews do have guts." Dean had gone upstairs with Secret Service agent Forrest Sorrells within about fifteen minutes after the shooting and participated in the questioning of Ruby. Upon Dean's testimony, Belli asked for a mistrial, on the grounds that Ruby's constitutional rights as a prisoner under arrest had been violated. Judge Brown overruled his motion (Statement of Facts, 529–530).

In 1966, the Court of Criminal Appeals of Texas overturned the verdict in the Ruby trial, due in part to Sergeant Dean's testimony. While Judge Brown had ruled Ruby's statement to Dean and Sorrells was part of the *res gestae* surrounding the crime, and therefore admissible, the court ruled it was not admissible. Presiding Judge Morrison wrote: "The test in this case is spontaneity and these facts do not fit the test. One who is cautious enough to inquire whether his answers to the questions to be propounded to him are to be released to the news media [as Mr. Ruby had asked of Mr. Sorrells] is not speaking spontaneously" (*J. Rubenstein, alias Jack Ruby, appellant v. The State of Texas, appellee*, No. 37900, 407 S.W. 2d 793, Court of Criminal Appeals of Texas, Oct. 5, 1966).

The defense started its presentation in the afternoon with an ex-stripper who testified about calling Jack Ruby on the telephone the day that Oswald was shot. Her testimony was intended to establish a reason for Ruby to be near the police station at the time. She stated that Ruby had gone to the Western Union office nearby to send her a money order. Nothing very relevant came from her testimony or from a couple of other witnesses who followed her.

The stripper was Karen Lynn Bennett, "Little Lynn," in her ninth month of pregnancy. In an incident that was unknown to the jury at the time but part of the "circus atmosphere" surrounding the trial, Ms. Bennett reportedly fainted in the hallway outside the courtroom when seven escaped prisoners, one of them brandishing a fake pistol fashioned out of soap and shoe polish, rushed past her. Belli's wife, Joy, pushed Ms. Bennett into a stairwell to protect her. The prisoners took two women hostage and led them out of the courthouse past newsmen and the crowd that had been attracted by the trial. Out-side, they released the hostages. Dramatic photos of the escape ap-peared in the newspapers. Five of the escapees were quickly captured, but two were not collared until the following day (Lehrer and Featherston, 1-A; "Frightened by jailbreak," 10-A).

Judge Brown disappointed the jury at 4:45 P.M. when he announced that the court would recess until 9:00 A.M. Monday. We had wanted to continue throughout the next day, Saturday. However, I'm sure that we twelve jurors were the only ones in that crowded courtroom who wanted to work Saturday. After all, we were the only ones except the defendant who would be locked up over the weekend. Looking at the defense and prosecution attorneys, they all appeared to need the long weekend to rest, and so did Judge Brown.

Unfortunately, when a capital case requires that a jury be locked up day after day, the jury gets impatient to hear more hours of testi-mony each day. Somehow, it didn't seem fair that we were required to spend twenty hours a day locked up and only four or so hours a day listening to testimony. It seemed as if too much time was being wasted, somewhere.

We now faced a long weekend of confinement. For me, it was the third such weekend. For most of the jury, it was their second. Only Aileen Shields and Louise Malone had not spent a previous weekend locked up. This weekend was spent loafing around our quarters listening to records and playing games. Allen McCoy had asked his wife to send him his portable stereo record player along with some of his favorite records. This was to result in the jury's only disagreement and it was carried out with much enthusiastic good humor. Allen favored classical music while Nell Tyler, Doug Sowell, several others, and I liked our music a bit lighter. Naturally several of us sent home for a couple of our own favorite records, such as Nat King Cole and Ray Charles. These records we played on Allen's record player, much to his displeasure. Allen seemed to be disgusted with our choice of music, and we in turn kidded him about his high-brow classical stuff. We relieved some of our tensions good-naturedly arguing over what music we were to listen to. When Allen would get outvoted, he would threaten to send his record player home because he was afraid our "junk" music might damage his stereo. Of course, everyone made a bigger thing of this disagreement in music than really existed.

Saturday morning, almost everyone slept until 8:00 or 9:00 A.M. and we didn't go out to breakfast until after 10:00 A.M. We walked the three blocks to the Dallas-Jefferson Coffee Shop for breakfast. After a leisurely breakfast, we stopped by a cleaning establishment where several of us had deposited clothes to be cleaned. With our cleaning in hand, we arrived back at our quarters around 11:30 A.M. Saturday morning, Bo escorted several of the men out to a local barbershop. These were the ones who had not gotten a haircut the previous Saturday. Saturday evening we again loaded into the familiar unmarked sheriff's cars for our journey to dinner at one of the suburban restaurants.

Sunday was a carbon copy of Saturday except that we did enjoy standing out on a street corner in back of the Dallas Hotel and watching workmen with a wrecking crane demolish a large multistory building. We watched this activity for more than an hour, and some of us could have enjoyed it longer but the women members did not find this as interesting as did we men. After this activity, we returned to our familiar cave of confinement.

Monday, 9 March, we sent word to Judge Brown, by Bo, that we could sit for much longer stretches and did not need long recesses. We made it plain that we were perfectly willing to spend longer hours on the job. The defense started that Monday morning off with an old friend of Ruby's childhood, ex-welterweight champion Barney Ross. Ross was followed by a female entertainer. Both testified that they had witnessed Ruby acting abnormally at one time or another.

One strong defense witness was Ike Pappas, a reporter, who was only a couple of feet away from Oswald when he was shot. Pappas stated that he was attempting to get a statement from Oswald and that he had turned his tape recorder on to record the statement, just prior to the shot being fired. The tape was played back to the jury, and there was no record of the statement ["You son of a bitch!"] that had been credited to Ruby in earlier testimony from the state's witnesses. Pappas stated that as close as he was to both Oswald and Ruby, he had not heard the words attributed to Ruby by the detectives in Friday's testimony.

Pappas was then a reporter for WNEW radio in New York City. He testified: "At the time of the shooting, I was holding what we call a pencil microphone. My proximity to the shooting was five feet. I believe, five or six feet." Of the Nagra tape recorder he was using, Pappas said, "It's perhaps the best, as far as quality and sensitivity, I would say." Pappas had tried to ask a question of Oswald almost simultaneously as Ruby was making his move. Belli asked, "Did you hear Jack Ruby say anything from your position?" Pappas replied, "I heard nothing before the shot went off." Pappas testified that after the shot, he heard Oswald moan twice and nothing more, other than the general shouts amid the confusion.

During cross-examination, Henry Wade asked Pappas about the microphone. "What I'm getting at, the mike won't pick up—you might get a noise or something, but you can't understand some six or eight feet away plain[ly] . . . isn't that right?" Pappas replied, "No, sir. I would say it would pick up quite clearly."

The tape Pappas played for the court was a copy of the master tape, and it had a couple of brief erasures. Pappas testified that the erasures had happened the day before as he was listening to the tape again and feeding parts of it to his station in New York for use in a broadcast story on the trial. He said he pressed the record button by mistake. He offered to have the master tape delivered from New York (Statement of Facts, 787, 795, 799, 801, 803, 804).

Fireworks really erupted in the courtroom in the afternoon during the testimony of Dr. Roy Schafer, a psychologist. There was a real battle over the right of the prosecution to ask Dr. Schafer, if in his opinion, Ruby knew the difference between right and wrong at the time of the shooting. The defense objected to the doctor offering such an opinion on the basis that he was a psychologist, and not qualified to give such an opinion. Their contention was that the doctor only performed specific tests that other medical doctors used to base their opinions upon. After several exchanges of volleys between the defense and the prosecution, the judge ordered us out of the courtroom until he could clear this matter up. Needless to say we would have enjoyed hearing the rest of the discussion but by law we could not. So we were retired while the judge met with the attorneys to hear their arguments and rule on whether or not to allow Dr. Schafer to testify without making a statement regarding Ruby's sanity.

After Belli questioned Dr. Schafer for an extended period of time, Assistant District Attorney Bill Alexander interjected: "May it please the court, at this time we want to object to all this. He has not asked the witness if he has an opinion as to the soundness or unsoundness of the defendant's mind. If he does not have an opinion, then this is needless." To which Belli responded, in exasperation, "Judge, may I conduct this my own way, and go into the tests and what he [Schafer] found? We're going to come to that [the issue of 'right from wrong'], and I assure the court, very thoroughly we'll come to that, even to the McNaughten Rule [upon which Texas law on insanity was based]." Judge Brown, perhaps becoming restless himself, asked Belli, "Counsel, how far off is it?" Belli said it would take another hour, and

Judge Brown allowed the testimony to continue.

After the questioning continued for awhile, Alexander again objected, on the same grounds as before. This time, Judge Brown told Belli, "The court's going to sustain you [Alexander] in that, counsel." Belli interjected, "Sustain him in what, Your Honor, first?" Judge Brown replied, "Whether or not the man [Ruby], under the McNaughten Rule, knew right from wrong. . . ."

As the debate continued, both sides agreed that the jury should not be listening to the heated discussion. "Let's take it out of the presence of the jury, because so help me, I'm going to make a record on this for some court, Your Honor, and I say that respectfully," Mr. Belli commented, more than hinting at a future appeal. Judge Brown then ordered the jury out.

With the jury out of the courtroom, Belli explained again that Dr. Schafer's testimony was building a "predicate" for testimony to come from psychiatrists who had examined Ruby. Judge Brown again said, "The court's going to sustain the state's objection to it, Mr. Belli." But then a very curious thing happened. The prosecution began to backpedal on its argument that Dr. Schafer must testify as to whether Ruby knew right from wrong. Assistant District Attorney Jim Bowie said, "We have no objection to going into it if they will assure us that some doctor, sometime, some place, and I hope in this courtroom, will say that he used it [Dr. Schafer's examination of Ruby] as the basis of his opinion." Judge Brown then asked, "Mr. Belli, are you going to connect it up?" Belli replied, "Certainly." When the judge agreed to let Belli continue his questioning of Dr. Schafer, Belli said triumphantly, "I believe my brother [referring to Bowie] is very concerned with the error that he has again led Your Honor into in striking this testimony," again apparently thinking ahead to an appeal (Statement of Facts, 871, 872, 876, 880, 883, 888, 895, 890).

We were eventually ushered back into the jury box where we heard Dr. Schafer's testimony, in which he stated that as a result of certain tests that he ran on Ruby, he believed that he possessed an abnormal mind, a mind capable of erratic and impulsive actions. At the conclusion of Dr. Schafer's testimony, Judge Brown recessed court until 9:00

A.M. Tuesday. Judge Brown had really cooperated with us. We didn't shut down for the night until 6:45 P.M. It was a good day for the jury, measured in hours of testimony heard.

"I came to the conclusion that he [Ruby] did have organic brain damage, and that the most likely specific nature of it was psychomotor epilepsy," Dr. Schafer testified. Schafer said he conducted a Rorschach test on Ruby which formed "a very important part of [his] final conclusions" and found "signs of confusion . . . tendencies toward incoherence and misuse of words . . . marked emotionality, emotional instability, impulsiveness, readiness towards reactions of anger of an explosive nature, and, in a number of major respects, a tying of the emotional impulsiveness and instability with irrational thinking."

Under cross-examination, Wade asked Dr. Schafer the question the prosecution had wanted the defense to ask. "Did you form an opinion [on whether Ruby knew right from wrong]?" "No," replied Dr. Schafer. Wade asked Dr. Schafer if it was true that it was rare for people with a high IQ to have psychomotor epilepsy, and Dr. Schafer agreed that it was. Dr. Schafer said Ruby's IQ was 109, higher than seventy-three percent of American men his age (Statement of Facts, 863, 872, 931).

Tuesday, 10 March, Dr. Martin L. Towler testified that in his opinion two sets of EEG (brain wave) tracings of Ruby's reflected abnormal patterns. Dr. Towler and Mr. Belli brought the tracings over to the ledge in front of the jury box so that each juror could see the tracings. They proceeded to thumb through each of the hundreds of pages of tracings a page at a time, stopping to point out to us the irregular patterns that would occasionally appear. This testimony and viewing continued for some time, long after they had made their point that the tracings were, at points, abnormal.

Dr. Towler, a specialist in neurology and psychiatry on the staff of the University of Texas Medical Branch at Galveston and a professor in the university's Department of Neurology and Psychiatry, had examined Ruby on Jan. 28–29 and had interviewed Ruby's sister and brother. The court had appointed Dr. Towler and two other doctors before the trial to conduct independent psychiatric exams on Ruby, and Dr. Towler had written a report on their findings. Dr. Towler testified extensively about Ruby's troubled personal history, which included numerous head injuries caused by fights and beatings. Dr. Towler said Ruby complained of painful "prickling sensations" in his head that Ruby called "spells." After having these spells, Ruby said, "I did not feel that I was there."

Dr. Towler testified: "On the basis of the history of 'spells' described by the subject as well as the abnormal electroencephalographic recordings, it is my opinion that the subject is suffering from a seizure disorder. This type of seizure disorder falls into the category of a psychomotor variant. This type of seizure phenomenon has recently been described by Dr. Frederic A. Gibbs, et al., in the December 1963 issue of *Neurology*, the official journal of the American Academy of Neurology." In the preceding, Dr. Towler seems to be reading from his Feb. 13 report to the court. Dr. Towler went on to say that a person suffering psychomotor seizures could act as an "automaton," without knowing what he's doing. Dr. Gibbs had written a letter in support of Dr. Towler's report, specifically his analysis of Ruby's EEG and his diagnosis of Ruby having symptoms of psychomotor variant mental illness, an affliction related to psychomotor epilepsy (Kaplan and Waltz 1965, 86–87). Belli had tried several times to enter the letter into the trial as evidence, but his efforts had been rejected by Judge Brown.

Wade, while cross-examining Dr. Towler, asked this rambling question: "Now, do you think a man in one of these fugue states [periods in which a person may commit unconscious acts], could find his way into the basement of the Dallas City Jail, slip past the policemen with a gun in his hand, 200 hundred people in the basement, and in that mob of people, fight his way through all of them and kill one person, and while killing him say, 'You son of a bitch?' Do you think that sounds like a person that didn't know what he was doing?" Dr. Towler was not rattled: "Of course, you know, I have no way of knowing whether there is a fugue state here or not. The behavior of an individual during a psychomotor seizure, or a fugue state, is unpredict-able" (Statement of Facts, 962, 977–978, 982–983, 984, 994–995, 1000–1001, 1044).

After Dr. Towler, we heard from Dr. Manfred Guttmacher, another highly recognized expert in the field of criminal psychiatry. For the first time, we heard a medical expert testify that in his opinion Ruby was not capable of knowing right from wrong or understanding the nature and consequences of his act at the time of the shooting. This was what it was all about, the McNaughten Rule, which under the law would establish sanity or insanity.

The McNaughten or M'Naughten rule is a standard for judging legal insanity which requires that either an offender did not know what he or she were doing, or that, if he or she did, that he or she did not know it was wrong (Schmalleger 1999). Under Texas law, it was the standard of guilt or innocence used by the jury in the trial of Jack Ruby. Ironically, an article that appeared within a week of the assassination of President Kennedy and the murder of Oswald questioned the appropriateness of the McNaughten Rule. "In increasing number, lawyers and judges are wondering whether justice needs a better guide. Says Psychiatrist Bernard L. Diamond, a member of a commission appointed by California Governor Pat Brown to study the state's criminal insanity laws: 'A person who is so mentally ill that he doesn't understand right from wrong would be a drooling idiot incapable of action'" ("Redefining Insanity" 1963, 54).

In another 1963 article, Drs. Franklin G. Ebaugh and John M. Macdonald were quoted: "Only the idiot, the grossly demented senile, or the severely delirious patient can be said to have no knowledge of right or wrong, and these persons seldom appear in the criminal courts." They recommended, instead, the concept of "diminishing responsibility" in which a murder charge would lead to a verdict of guilty of manslaughter and the sentence would be left to the judge's discretion ("Nobody is hardly ever mad enough . . ." 1963, 57).

Dr. Guttmacher's opinion was the first significant credit established by the defense in its medical case to establish that Ruby was in a state of psychomotor epilepsy, and thereby did not know what he was doing at the time Oswald was shot. During cross-examination, the prosecution did very little in the way of discrediting Dr. Guttmacher's testimony.

During the cross-examination, Dr. Guttmacher testified, "I think he [Ruby] had psychomotor epilepsy. There is no question of that." But while Causey felt the prosecution did little to discredit Dr. Guttmacher's testimony, it seems possible that Wade was able to cast doubt on Dr. Guttmacher's diagnosis in other jurors' minds, based on this confusing exchange:

Wade: Well, isn't your psychomotor epilepsy based on some brain damage?

Guttmacher: That's right. Brain malfunction could be congenital, it can be—there is no exact knowledge as to what in many cases has caused the malfunctioning. . . .

Wade: Is there any brain damage there in the sense of the [Ruby's] electroencephalogram?

Guttmacher: No, not in the sense of the electroencephalogram, no.

Wade: And your brain damage on psychomotor epilepsy will show up on it?

Guttmacher: That's right, sir . . . I based the diagnosis on hereditary instability. His [Ruby's] mother was a sick woman. That has a great deal of influence, the type of environment in which the child grows up.

Wade: The mother having paranoia schizophrenia, would that cause psychomotor epilepsy?

Guttmacher: I wouldn't think so. I don't think you could make a direct cause of it, no.

Wade: Well, you've read all the books on the subject?

Guttmacher: No, I haven't by any means.

Wade: Haven't you?

Guttmacher: No.

Wade: We don't think this is admissible, your honor, and we object to it.

Later, under further cross-examination by Assistant District Attorney Bill Alexander, Dr. Guttmacher testified: "I don't think we have data on which we can tell whether this man was in a psychomotor epileptic attack at the time, but it could have occurred in a person of his makeup under that degree of stress, without being at that moment a psychomotor epileptic attack." Dr. Guttmacher, pressed by Mr. Alexander as to exactly what condition might have caused Ruby to shoot Oswald, said, "I think it is best called 'episodic dyscontrol.'"

On this complex topic it should be noted that the other defense psychiatric witnesses, including Dr. Frederic A. Gibbs, recognized as the "founder of electroencephalography," also testified that Ruby apparently suffered from psychomotor epilepsy or psychomotor variant (Statement of Facts, 1084–1085, 1131).

Judge Brown recessed court after the close of Dr. Guttmacher's testimony until 9:00 A.M. the next day. This had been another good day for hearing testimony, not as good as Monday but still a good day. We felt sure that if we could hear several full days of testimony that we would certainly have to arrive at the end of the trial sometime soon. We were to have a good surprise the next morning. But tonight we were a hungry group of jurors and so we again were driven to a suburban restaurant for dinner. It was during this evening meal that some of the jurors' families were told where we were to have dinner and they also ate at the cafeteria, but, of course, at separate tables. Again there was not one single exchange of words between the jurors and their families, only waves and smiles, but this time without the restraint of a formal courtroom. Even these remote contacts with their families helped to brighten the daily routine of the confined jurors. We all enjoyed our dinner very much.

Wednesday, 11 March, I awoke early and as I lay in bed, I counted the days that I had occupied my small room. It was my twenty-first day of confinement. I wondered how much longer it would take for us to hear all the testimony, the rebuttals, the summations, the judge's charge to us, and most of all, once this was done, would we twelve jurors all have the same convictions as to the innocence or guilt of Mr. Ruby. And if the decision was to be guilt, could we agree on the punishment? It seemed to me that there was certain to be several more nights for us in this "hotel."

The biggest shock of the trial came about 9:15 A.M. March 11, when Mr. Belli rose to his feet and told the court, "The defense rests." I'm not sure what any of us expected that Wednesday morning, but I'm sure that none of us expected the defense to rest so soon. As surprised as the jury was, I don't think we were any more surprised than was the prosecution. I looked over at the prosecution table to see what they were going to do now, and I noticed that they appeared to be taken completely by surprise. At any rate, we were ushered from the jury box and back up the stairs to our day quarters where we were to remain for the next one and one half hours before being recalled.

Why did the defense rest at this point? In his book, *Dallas Justice*, Belli wrote: "We had not, of course, proved beyond a reasonable doubt that Ruby was insane at the time of the shooting. But one of the few sensible aspects of the prevailing rule on legal insanity is that the defense need counter the normal presumption that a defendant is sane by no more than preponderance of the evidence. To establish insanity, the defense must do more than raise the possibility, but it does not have the same burden of proof beyond a reasonable doubt by which the prosecution must establish guilt. If the weight of the evidence can tip the presumption of sanity ever so slightly over the line toward the likelihood of insanity, the job is done. . . . So, taking a chance, we came into court the next morning, and before the jury had even settled in their seats, I rose and told Judge Brown, 'Your Honor, the defense rests'" (Belli 1964, 202–203). However, it seems clear the Ruby trial jury did not believe that a "preponderance of the evidence" established that Ruby suffered from psychomotor epilepsy.

We were reseated in the jury box for only about an hour after the defense rested. The prosecution commenced its medical rebuttal with Dr. Sheff Olinger. He concurred with the defense that Ruby's brain tracings were consistent with those found in psychomotor epilepsy; however, he could not reach a diagnosis of psychomotor epilepsy from the tracings.

Dr. Olinger, a neurologist with the Dallas Neurology Clinic, was considered the regional authority on electroencephalography. He testified that Ruby's EEGs of Jan. 29 indicated no organic brain damage. Under questioning from Wade, Dr. Olinger gave this testimony concerning the EEGs: "I should say that the test itself is a rather non-specific test . . . and did not indicate any particular clinical disease. The significance of these changes [in Ruby's brain waves], which I will term minor, is indeterminate to me." Later asked about Dr. Towler's report, Dr. Olinger said, "The reports of Dr. Towler's examination and the electroencephalogram combined would not allow me to make a diagnosis of psychomotor epilepsy. I should say that it is possible to have psychomotor epilepsy and a normal electroencephalogram. But I couldn't establish this diagnosis on the basis of either of these areas, or both combined." Asked by Wade, "Do you agree with Dr. Towler's report?" Olinger replied, "I disagree with it."

In his cross-examination of Dr. Olinger, Belli attempted to discredit his disagreement with Dr. Towler and Dr. Gibbs over the conclusiveness of the EEGs: "[Dr. Gibbs], of all people, has done the definitive work on encephalograms in the United States, hasn't he? Isn't he called the 'father of electroencephalography' like George Washington is called the 'father of his county?'" Dr. Olinger was not overwhelmed. "Well, I'm not sure about that," he replied (Statement of Facts, 1208, 1212, 1214–1215, 1216, 1220).

After lunch, we heard from Dr. Robert L. Stubblefield, who had, along with Dr. Towler, previously examined Ruby. At the time of this examination he had considered Ruby to be sane. He further stated that based upon all the medical evidence that he was familiar with, Ruby did know the difference between right and wrong and the nature and consequence of his act at the time Oswald was shot. While agreeing with the defense that Ruby was somewhat unstable, he would not accept Dr. Frederic A. Gibbs' concept that he was in a fugue state or psychomotor variant state.

Dr. Stubblefield was professor and chairman of the Department of Psychiatry at Southwestern Medical School in Dallas, and chief of surgery at Dallas's Parkland Hospital. He was a diplomate of the American Board of Psychiatry and Neurology. At the request of the court, Dr. Stubblefield, Dr. Towler, Dr. Tynus McNeel, and Dr. John Holbrook had examined Ruby on Jan. 27. Dr. Stubblefield testified that he found Ruby neurologically normal, and that, if the testimony of the police who arrested Ruby was accurate, he probably knew the difference in right and wrong. In his cross-examination of Dr. Stubblefield, Belli attempted to show that Dr. Stubblefield had not disagreed with the report on Ruby's mental state written by Dr. Towler in consultation with Dr. Stubblefield and Dr. Holbrook. "And you read his report and his clinical opinion, did you not?" Belli asked. "That is correct," Dr. Stubblefield replied. "I did not necessarily endorse his clinical opinion." Belli persisted, "All right, but you didn't disagree with it." Dr. Stubblefield responded, "Not in that letter. That letter is worded very carefully" (Statement of Facts, 1257, 1260, 1264, 1266, 1273).

Following Dr. Stubblefield, the prosecution paraded several other medical doctors—John T. Holbrook, Peter Kellaway and A. Earl Walker—all of whom agreed that the Ruby brain tracings were somewhat abnormal. None of the doctors would accept the remote possibility of the Gibbs concept of psychomotor variant. After we had heard these doctors testify, the prosecution rested its medical rebuttal. After we heard several defense surrebuttal witnesses testify, the court was recessed for the day.

Dr. Holbrook, a psychiatrist with the Beverly Hills Clinic in Dallas and former resident psychiatrist at Parkland Hospital, testified: "I felt that he [Ruby] did know right from wrong, and he knew the nature and consequences of his act at that time." He had examined Ruby on five occasions. Dr. Kellaway was president of the American

Electroencephalography Society and professor and director of the Laboratory of Clinical Encephalography at Baylor University College of Medicine in Houston. He testified that he examined 2,400 to 2,500 EEGs per year. In cross-examination, Belli pointed out that defense witness Dr. Towler studied 4,000 EEGs per year. Dr. Kellaway testified that nothing in Ruby's EEGs would lead him to a diagnosis of psychomotor epilepsy, and further commented that the EEG was a diagnostic aid and could not, by itself, provide such a diagnosis. Dr. Walker was neurosurgeon-in-charge at Johns Hopkins Hospital in Baltimore and testified that the EEGs were not indicative of psychomotor epilepsy (Statement of Facts, 1285, 1289, 1340, 1341, 1343–1344, 1346, 1358, 1360–1361).

Thursday, 12 March, was spent mostly in listening to a rehash of testimony already heard. We heard from some ten or twelve additional defense witnesses. [These witnesses testified as part of the rebuttal and surrebuttal phase of the trial, after both sides had officially rested their cases], the most significant of whom was Ruby's rabbi, Hillel E. Silverman, who testified of witnessing Ruby's abnormal behavior at one time or another. Rabbi Silverman stated that in his opinion there were times when Ruby did not know the difference between right and wrong and that he didn't feel that Ruby knew the difference at the present time.

Silverman, the rabbi of Shearith Israel in Dallas, testified that Ruby seemed "to be in a sort of trance" at services on the Friday night of President Kennedy's assassination. Once, Silverman said, Ruby came to him upset that Ruby's sister refused to sit with him in the synagogue because of an argument between them. The rabbi then discussed the problem with Ruby's sister. "In the conversation, she told me it wasn't only a misunderstanding or argument, but that he had shoved her, pushed her and actually struck her, and that's the reason she couldn't sit next to him at the services. Jack had no memory of that when I called him back. He didn't remember that at all." Silverman recalled that once Ruby appeared at the rabbi's home with several dogs. "Suddenly, he began to cry. He said, 'I'm unmarried.

[Pointing to a dog] This is my wife, these are my children.'" Silverman said within five or ten minutes, Ruby "forgot about it completely and went on to another subject." The rabbi said he considered Ruby "very unstable, very emotional, very erratic," and said he believed Ruby did not know right from wrong when he shot Oswald (Statement of Facts, 1459, 1452–1453, 1454).

The defense rested its surrebuttal about midafternoon and the prosecution started its surrebuttal. The prosecution came across with three good, impressive medical experts, Drs. Robert Schwab, Francis Forster and Roland McKay. Dr. Forster stated that he had been President Eisenhower's doctor. All three doctors stated that they disagreed with the defense diagnosis that Ruby suffered from psychomotor epilepsy, based on the diagnosis from the brain tracings.

About 5:00 P.M., real fireworks exploded when the defense announced that they were bringing the eminent Dr. Gibbs down from Chicago to testify. We had probably heard more about this man than any other man excluding Jack Ruby himself since the first day of testimony. The prosecution, somewhat stunned by this announcement, objected to any delay in waiting for a defense witness who would not arrive in town until early morning. After several minutes of bickering and shouting between the prosecution and the defense, the judge ordered Bo to retire the jury. At the time we left the jury box, we thought that we would be returning in a few minutes to hear additional testimony. However, after several minutes, Judge Brown ruled in favor of the defense to allow court to recess and await the arrival the next day of Dr. Gibbs. A little while later, Bo came up the stairs to our quarters and advised us that court had recessed for the day and that we could go to dinner.

Belli was questioning Dr. Roland McKay, a psychiatrist and prosecution witness, asking him to give his opinion on Dr. Gibbs' letter in support of Dr. Towler's diagnosis of Ruby's mental state. Assistant District Attorney Bill Alexander was again objecting to Belli's attempt to somehow introduce Dr. Gibbs' letter into evidence, when Joe Tonahill, Belli's assistant, suddenly trumpeted: "We assure you

Dr. Gibbs will be here to testify to the contents of that letter, Judge."
Belli, in apparent surprise, asked Tonahill, "Did you just call him?"
Tonahill responded, "Yes. We assure you. He will be here." Judge Brown
again sustained the prosecution's objection to the letter.

Later, Mr. Tonahill told the judge, "Dr. Gibbs will be here at
midnight, Your Honor, and we'll put him on first thing in the morning." Judge Brown, fast running out of patience, replied, "No, we're
going to close this case tonight, gentlemen. I told you today we
were going to go on through the testimony till we finished it." Belli
responded incredulously, "I've been trying to get this man, Judge.
And he's refused to come into the courtroom, he's never been in the
courtroom, till he's been reading some of this stuff in the newspapers. . . ." Mr. Wade interjected, "Your Honor, we object," and, at
that point, Judge Brown announced, "Retire the jury." The argument continued in the judge's chambers, before Brown announced,
"There will be one witness in the morning" (Statement of Facts,
1625, 1629, 1630).

Friday, 13 March, I again woke early and, as I had done many
times during the past few days, I began going over the testimony in my
mind. I wondered how significant Dr. Gibbs' testimony would be.
Despite all the well-qualified and eminent professional medical experts
that we had heard testify, the actual conclusion was going to be our
own. No one outside the twelve jurors could weigh the evidence we
had heard and act upon it. How I wished that either one side or the
other would present evidence that would make the final decision easier.
Up to this point, Friday morning, the defense had not actually convinced me Ruby was insane to the point that he didn't know the difference between right and wrong at the time he shot Oswald. The defense had never argued that Ruby didn't shoot Oswald, only that he
didn't know what he was doing at the time because he was in a fugue
state, or in a form of psychomotor epilepsy at the time. Granted, there
had been good evidence presented that such a phenomenon was possible, but on the other hand it had been challenged just as effectively
that it was highly improbable that this was the case. I knew that a man
is innocent until proven guilty and sane until proven insane. Now the

state had proven without challenge that Ruby was guilty of physically shooting Oswald to death. I wondered if the other members of the jury were weighing the evidence day-by-day as I had been. I wondered how they were viewing the testimony to this point. Were they, as I was, waiting and praying for that big break to come in the case that would make our decision a little easier? Maybe we would get that big break, at least from what we had been led to expect, from Dr. Gibbs. He just might be the one who would swing the scale of justice one way or the other.

At last we heard from Dr. Gibbs. He was a distinguished, tall, graying, typically professional man. He very strongly substantiated the defense's case that Ruby's brain wave tracing did very certainly indicate psychomotor variant patterns and that, in his opinion, Ruby's pattern suggested a very rare form of epilepsy. For what seemed to me like the fourth time during the trial, we were shown close-ups of the voluminous EEG tracings while Dr. Gibbs went through it again under Mr. Belli's close and directed questioning. Mr. Belli expertly conducted the questioning of Dr. Gibbs and was finished with him in less than half an hour.

Assistant District Attorney Mr. Bill Alexander cross-examined Dr. Gibbs without much success in shaking his medical credibility. Then Mr. Alexander dropped the bomb on Dr. Gibbs. He asked him if he had an opinion as to whether Ruby knew the difference between right and wrong and the nature and consequences of his act at the time that he shot Oswald. Dr. Gibbs's answer absolutely floored me, because I had felt certain that he would offer his opinion to support the defense. He stated, without hesitation, "I have no opinion." I asked myself, What had been the point? Why had this eminent professional man traveled all this distance just to state that he had no opinion as to Ruby's sanity at the time of the shooting? The mere fact that he had added his weight to the defense that the EEG tracings indicated psychomotor variant, a rare type of epilepsy, was existent in Ruby did not seem worth the trip. Needless to say, I had expected more from this great man. Perhaps I had expected too much. When Dr. Gibbs left the stand, we had heard the last of the witnesses in the Jack Ruby trial.

Dr. Gibbs came to Dallas at his own expense and testified for the defense because he was displeased with what he read about the testimony concerning psychomotor variant epilepsy. He had thus far resisted all attempts by the defense to convince him he should testify. The eminent physician testified that he examined EEG tracings of Ruby made by defense psychiatrist Dr. Martin L. Towler and diagnosed his condition as psychomotor variant epilepsy: "I determined that Jack Ruby had a particular, very rare type of epilepsy, one that does not manifest itself usually in convulsive seizures but in various other ways. . . .The pattern occurs in only one-half percent of epileptics, and is a very distinctive and unusual epileptic pattern." Dr. Gibbs testified that with this type of psychomotor epilepsy, a person frequently exhibits "lack of emotional control, convulsive or excessive types of behavior." Asked by Belli, if the condition was "unmistakable" in Ruby's EEG, Dr. Gibbs replied, "It is."

During cross-examination, Assistant District Attorney Bill Alexander asked Dr. Gibbs: "Do you have an opinion from your electroencephalogram [EEG] as to whether Jack Ruby knew the difference between right and wrong and understood the nature and consequences of his acts on November 24?" Gibbs responded, "I have no opinion." Alexander concluded his questioning of Dr. Gibbs by asking, "Doctor, from this EEG tracing, you cannot say whether Jack Ruby knew the difference between right and wrong, or understood the nature and consequences of his act, can you?" Dr. Gibbs replied, "No, I cannot" (Statement of Facts, 1641, 1645–1646, 1650, 1660, 1663).

The jury was retired after Dr. Gibbs' testimony ended at about 10:30 A.M. while the court prepared to hear the summations from the defense and the prosecution. We expected that we would be out of the jury box only a half-hour to an hour before commencing to hear the summations. Actually it was 8:00 P.M. before we were once again seated in the jury box. We asked Bo what was keeping us out of the box for such an incredibly long time, and he could only tell us that the judge and attorneys were preparing the charge that the judge would give to us at the beginning of the summations. It was a long and confused afternoon for us, because we were not informed very well as to what to expect in regard to how long this courtroom activity might require. I never did fully learn why all of this shouldn't have been completed in an orderly manner rather than causing complete disruption of the trial process for almost ten hours before resuming at dark. We the jury, most of all wanted to get this case tried and found it most discomforting to experience this delay without knowing why.

The delay was caused by the strenuous objections of the defense to the charge—the judge's instructions to the jury. Judge Brown agreed to allow the defense to prepare written objections to the charge. Assistant defense attorney Phil Burleson dictated a thirty-six-page document containing 134 objections to the judge's instructions. Meanwhile, the other attorneys remained in the courtroom deciding procedures for the final arguments. One of the key objections was that rather than the McNaughten rule, another legal principal, the "Durham test" (Was the crime a product of a mental disease?) should have been applied. This would have been contrary to Texas law, but the objection was included with an eye cocked toward appeal. Another objection was that the charge ignored the subtleties of the medical testimony the defense had presented. Finally, the judge read the objections of the defense to the charge, made a few minor changes and recalled the jury. By this time, it was 8:04 P.M. (Kaplan and Waltz 1965, 306–307)

In his charge to the jury, Judge Brown told the jurors: "Every person charged with an offense is presumed to be sane . . . until the contrary is shown by proof. If . . . the guilt of the defendant has been established beyond a reasonable doubt, it devolves on the defendant to establish his insanity at the time of committing the act in order to excuse himself from legal responsibility . . . If the defendant was not of sound mind but was affected with insanity and such affection, if any, was the cause of the alleged act . . . then he ought to be acquitted . . . but this unsoundness of mind or affection of insanity, if any, must be of such a degree as to obliterate the sense of right and wrong. . . . It is not necessary that the insanity of the defendant should be established beyond a reasonable doubt. It is sufficient if it be estab-

lished to your satisfaction by the weight or preponderance of the
evidence. . . ." (Kaplan and Waltz 1965, 308–319)

When at long last we were once again seated in the jury box for
what was to be, except for short recesses, the next to last time, we
heard Judge Brown read the charge to the jury. The charge is the legal
ground rules that a jury may use in a particular case, based on the
evidence heard. Of course, there was the innocence or guilty verdict,
each with mitigating circumstances. Also, there was the degree of punishment latitude that was open to us if we found him guilty. Judge
Brown used about twenty minutes going over this charge to us. After
Judge Brown finished reading the charge to us, the prosecution commenced their final arguments of the summation with Mr. Alexander
leading off. Alexander was followed by a defense argument from Phil
Burleson. He was followed by [assistant district attorney] Frank Watts
for the prosecution, who was followed by Joe Tonahill for the defense,
and Jim Bowie for the prosecution. Finally, the lead attorneys spoke,
Mr. Belli for the defense and Mr. Wade for the state. Each of these men
presented an intelligent and persuasive argument for his particular side.

When finally, the last of the arguments had been presented and
District Attorney Wade sat down, it was one minute past 1:00 A.M.
Saturday, 14 March. Judge Brown asked us if we wanted to commence
deliberations then or wait until after we had a night's sleep. We elected
to sleep first.

In my layman's opinion, our American judicial trial-by-jury system
is at its weakest during the final arguments by counsel. For five hours,
from 8:00 P.M. until 1:00 A.M., we listened intently as one eloquent
attorney after another pleaded both intelligently and emotionally before us. Each member of the team retraced the evidence as they had
previously presented it to us, while belittling that which their opponents had presented. The final arguments in a criminal case are
designed to sway the jury one way or another with pure emotion, with
the eloquence of a college debate team. I wonder just how many mis-
carriages of justice have been handed down due to an imbalance of
eloquent emotional persuasiveness of counsel, either on the part of the
defense or the prosecution. I do not believe that there was an imbal-

ance of this talent on either side during the Ruby trial. On the contrary, Mr. Belli and his defense team presented a very emotional appeal for us to free Ruby so that he could be given the proper psychiatric care. Mr. Wade and his prosecution staff emotionally appealed for us to give the death penalty to an infamous, publicity-seeking, cold-blooded killer, as they painted Ruby.

Excerpts from the closing arguments of Belli and Wade:

Belli: "When they look back at us forty, eighty years from now, when they look back at us and see how we sat here and tried to look into the brain of a sick man here, and I can't find it in my heart that you want the blood of this man on your hands, this sick man, or that you want one year of his time. . . . But you cannot find this sick man guilty of anything. It would be an incongruity to compromise and say one year, two years, five years. . . . You can't arrogate unto yourselves, you good jurors in this good town, the right to put a sick man in jail for six months, or to put a stigma on him by a suspended sentence."

Wade: "To turn this man loose, you would set civilization back a century, you would set it back to barbarianism, you would set it back to lynch law, and say that, 'Anybody that I decided should be killed, I can kill.' Jack Ruby was a glory seeker. . . . He wanted the limelight; he wanted publicity; he wanted heroism and fame; and wanted to go down in history as the man that killed an alleged assassin. And my question to you, ladies and gentlemen, what would you want the history books to say about you? Do you want them to say that you tried this case and slapped a man on the wrist and gave him a little penitentiary sentence? . . . Jack Ruby, and his murder, were the judge, jury and executioner. Now, he and his lawyers ask you for mercy, sympathy and compassion" (Statement of Facts, 124, 125, 154, 160, 165).

After we left the courtroom that early morning and returned to our sleeping quarters, most of us went directly to bed. As for me, I went to bed but not to sleep. I must have lain awake for more than an hour going over and over all the testimony in my mind before falling asleep.

Saturday morning, 14 March, we arose a little later than on previous days and went out to breakfast at the Dallas-Jefferson Hotel. While we didn't seem to rush through breakfast, we didn't linger over coffee either. We returned to the courthouse and up the stairs to our deliberation chambers a few minutes past 9:00 A.M. While I was in the bathroom, the rest of the jury voted and elected me jury foreman. I wouldn't accept this vote when I was not present, so it was retaken but with the same results. It was probably my seniority that brought this responsibility to me. I had been the first juror selected and had, of course, been present to greet each of the succeeding jurors when they joined our group. I had voted for Allen McCoy to be foreman.

As foreman of the jury, my first official act was to emphasize to the other members the importance and the solemnity of the task before us. I asked for a couple of minutes of complete silence so that each juror could search his or her own mind, and if the juror desired, ask divine direction in arriving at a decision. I personally said a short, silent prayer, and I suppose several of the others may have done likewise. I had never before sat on a jury of any kind, and, therefore, I didn't have any formulated idea as to how a foreman was supposed to perform. But I reasoned that it was my responsibility to organize and direct the collective reasoning of the other eleven members in a systematic analysis of the evidence. I took a pen and paper and jotted down what I thought were the issues that we had to decide, and read them to the other jurors, asking for their opinions as to whether or not I had left out an important issue.

It was our unanimous thinking that the first issue we had to decide was this: Did Jack Ruby in fact actually shoot Lee Harvey Oswald as charged? If we agreed to the first issue in the affirmative, then this was the second issue open to us: Was Jack Ruby legally sane at the time of the shooting? If this second issue was agreed to in the affirmative, then the third issue would be: Is Jack Ruby legally sane at the present time? An affirmative agreement here would bring on the fourth issue: Was there malice aforethought (premeditation) in Ruby's mind at the time of the shooting? The punishment was the final issue if we found the first four issues to be affirmative. Judge Brown's charge to us had given us options, depending upon the evidence, from a suspended sentence to death.

Once we had agreed on the plan of deliberation, which took about fifteen minutes, we started right down the sequential order of the issues. I asked all members of the jury if there was any of the testimony that anyone wished to hear again. There were two or three weak questions put forth that other members of the jury quickly clarified to the satisfaction of the juror who had asked the question. Then I asked the jury if there was anyone who wanted to discuss the first issue prior to a vote being taken. All agreed to vote. There were twelve affirmatives to issue number one. All agreed that Jack Ruby did actually shoot Lee Harvey Oswald.

I then read the second issue to the jury and asked them if anyone needed a point cleared up or to discuss this issue before taking a vote. Every juror was ready to vote on Ruby's sanity at the time of the shooting. I had felt that surely there would be doubt about this and figured this would lead to some discussion. The vote was unanimous, that Ruby was sane at the time of the shooting. This cleared the way for the third issue. Once again I asked if anyone wanted to discuss this issue before we voted. Once again there was silence. Everyone seemingly was ready to vote. Twelve ballots came back agreeing that Ruby was legally sane at the present time.

The fourth issue brought forth the first request that we discuss the issue before taking a vote. The evidence pertaining to the establishment of malice, along with the evidence against malice, was discussed. After a few minutes of discussing this issue, I asked if there was anyone not yet ready to vote on the question of malice. The silence indicated that a vote was ready. Once again, there were twelve unanimous ballots voting yes to malice. By this time, we had been in deliberation about one hour and fifteen minutes and we were down to the last issue to be decided, but the most important one of all, punishment.

Before we voted on the final issue concerning the fate of Jack Ruby, I asked the jury once again if there was anything that anyone wanted to discuss prior to taking this important vote. Several jurors spoke up in favor of immediately taking the vote. Not one juror asked for additional discussions. I then asked each juror to write down the sentence that he or she felt should be assessed Ruby based on the evidence we had heard. I asked them to take their time and not to make a hasty decision since a man's life was at stake. Twelve paper ballots were passed to me at the north end of the long deliberation table. I unfolded each ballot one at a time. The first ballot was death; the second ballot was death; the third ballot was death; the fourth ballot was life in prison; the fifth was death; the sixth was death; the seventh was death; the eighth was death; the ninth was death; the tenth was for sixty years in prison; the eleventh vote was death; the twelfth vote, my vote, was life in prison. There it was: seventy-five percent of the jurors had voted to give Ruby death on the very first vote.

I admitted to the other jurors that I had voted for life and stated my reasons for so doing. I had felt from the very early stages of the trial that Ruby was most probably a mentally unstable individual, a social deviant, a personality obsessed with notoriety who with certain stimuli might become violent. Several of my fellow jurors quickly pointed out to me that I had not hesitated or wavered in my vote that he was and is legally sane. To this, I could only agree. I was certain, then and now, that Ruby did assuredly know the difference between right and wrong at the time he shot Oswald.

However, I felt that there should have been more latitude within the law as it would apply to an unstable personality than there was within the McNaughten Rule. If there was, then it had not been properly brought out within the evidence. To me, it looked as though we, the jury, were on a tightrope with no place to go but to the death sentence for Ruby. One of the jurors admitted to the sentence of sixty years on the thinking that to a man of Ruby's personality, this was a more severe sentence than death. The other juror who voted life along with me never chose to disclose his or her identity.

After we had discussed the idea of an unstable but legally sane individual for several minutes and explored what was open to us by virtue of the judge's charge to us, I asked if everyone was ready to take another vote. All agreed that they were. The second ballot came in, ten votes for death and two for life in prison. I had not changed my vote, although I was convinced that there could be no less sentence than death based on what evidence we had heard, how we had voted on the first four issues, and the charge that we had to work with. In actuality, I was deliberately attempting to slow down what I felt was to be the ultimate sentence of death, trying to allow each juror more time to challenge his own conscience that it was the right decision.

We set about discussing the sentence for several minutes. Several of the jurors were getting a little disgruntled with my reluctance to agree unequivocally to the death sentence and were in a hurry to take a third vote. I was reminded that each of us had been qualified on the death sentence, prior to our acceptance on the jury. We had each testified that we could assess the death penalty where there was proof beyond a reasonable doubt that the defendant was guilty of murder with malice. They quickly pointed out that I had also voted yes on the issue of malice. I could never disagree with any of the arguments offered by my fellow jurymen trying to persuade me to vote the death penalty. I wanted to make as certain as I could that each of them was convinced of their own mind before I allowed myself to seemingly be converted to their decision. It was a few minutes after 11:00 A.M. when I asked for the third vote that was to decide the fate of Jack Ruby. Quickly all twelve ballots were collected and unfolded one by one. Twelve ballots read—DEATH.

Authors John Kaplan and Jon R. Waltz (1965, 338–339) offered this account of the deliberations, which varies only slightly from Causey's account: "The first order of business was to select their foreman and this was done with dispatch. The obvious candidate was Max Causey, the senior juror, who had impressed all as stable, thoughtful, and conscientious. Causey was elected by acclamation. . . . Different jurors have given somewhat different accounts [of the deliberations] and the majority has refused any comment at all. . . . Causey stated, 'As I see it the first question we have to decide is guilt or innocence—in other words, whether the defendant was sane or insane at the time of the crime.' With very little discussion, a secret ballot was taken on this issue and after about half the jurors counted the slips of paper with him, Causey announced, 'We are unanimous that the defendant was sane.'

The jurors . . . moved on to the question of whether the murder was with or without malice. After about fifteen minutes of discussion, one of the jurors suggested a ballot on this issue. The jurors all concurred and a few moments later it was announced that 'We're all agreed it was murder with malice.' Then the jurors moved on to the question of sentence. Preliminary discussion made it clear that the only issue was whether the verdict would be death or life imprisonment. The deliberations were careful and without acrimony. Some felt that Ruby was unstable and provoked and that executing him would do no good. The majority talked in terms of deterrence and the fact that they had promised that they would not oppose the death penalty in a proper case. The single factor mentioned most was that Ruby had shot a manacled, defenseless man.

The first ballot on the sentence showed eight of the twelve for death. Several more ballots brought the total up to eleven. Fifteen minutes more of discussion and the one holdout wavered. A final ballot was held and Causey announced, 'We are all agreed.' It had taken, in all, two hours and nineteen minutes. . . ."

I filled in the verdict form that Judge Brown had given us and signed the verdict, as foreman of the jury. I then walked down the so familiar stairs to the large door at the foot of the stairs that separated us from the courtroom. Bo Mabra answered my knock by opening the door. I informed him that we had reached a verdict. Bo said that he would have to call the judge to come to the courtroom and that it might take awhile for the court to assemble. While we waited for the court to assemble we drank coffee and Cokes. Some members of our number paced anxiously back and forth around the room.

It was about ten minutes past noon when Bo came back up the stairs and advised us that all was ready for us to return to the box with our verdict. I asked all members of the jury to pledge that they would not in any manner disclose to any news media the specific particulars of our deliberations. I felt that since we were not experts on the law there was always a chance that our discussions during deliberation might possibly have led to a legal question pertaining to a mistrial. I do not feel that anything we discussed could have led to grounds for a mistrial. However, to be on the completely safe side, if no one talked, then there could not possibly ever be grounds for a mistrial due to jury misconduct. All members of the jury agreed that this was the best policy to follow. It was further agreed that each of us should look directly at the defendant during the reading of the verdict. Later I read that Mr. Belli had accused this jury of not being able to face Ruby with the verdict and that not one member of the jury ever looked at him. This was not the case.

It was 12:20 P.M. when we filed into the jury box. The courtroom was packed with spectators standing around the walls. Judge Brown asked us if we had reached a verdict. We nodded our heads in the affirmative. Bo Mabra came over to the jury box, and I handed him the signed verdict, which he carried over to Judge Brown. Judge Brown slowly glanced over the verdict before he read it aloud to the court: "We the jury find the defendant guilty with malice, as charged, and affix his punishment at death."

I looked directly at Ruby during the reading of the verdict, and I have confidence that the other members of the jury did likewise. There was no visible emotional change in the defendant. He was ushered out immediately by the deputies who had guarded him all during this trial. Mr. Belli went into a screaming rage, ridiculing us for having handed down such an unjust verdict.

Belli shouted, "May I thank the jury for a victory for bigotry and injustice! Don't worry, Jack, we'll appeal this to a court outside Dallas where there is justice and due process of law! I hope the people of Dallas are proud of this jury!" (Belli 1964, 257)

I felt at the time that Mr. Belli's conduct was most unethical and below the dignity of a professional man of his esteem. Simultaneous with this, pandemonium broke loose in the courtroom as cameramen and newsmen climbed over tables and chairs and up the walls to get their cameras and microphones close to Mr. Belli and Mr. Wade. During this uproar, Judge Brown was thanking us for the service we rendered as jurors and dismissed us.

Bo ushered us up the stairs to wait in the deliberation room for the last time while the courtroom excitement subsided and the hallways were cleared. We delayed about fifteen minutes prior to making our final exit from the deliberation room that had been my daily habitat for the past three and one-half weeks. We returned to our night quarters and quickly packed our bags in preparation for going home. Everyone was eager to get home and to be rejoined with their families. We took turns on Bo's phone calling our families. When I called my wife, it was the first time in twenty-four days that I had been able to speak to her. I made plans with her that we would leave home immediately after I arrived in order that I would not have to face any newsmen for questions that I didn't want to answer. She agreed that we would go out of town to my father's farm and spend the night in hopes to avoid all contact with newsmen.

Sheriff Decker had suggested that his deputies drive us all home in the unmarked cars since there was a huge mob completely surrounding the building. Newsmen were all over the area trying to get a scoop by interviewing a member of the jury. The huge assembly of spectators gathered outside was most outspoken about its feelings. Many agreed with the verdict and many others disagreed just as strongly. To make matters worse, there was a St. Patrick's Day parade downtown and many spectators had come to the area to see the parade as well as to chance a meeting with a juror.

We all took our last ride down the elevator, this time going to the dock where prisoners are unloaded. Here, the deputies' cars were waiting to speed us to our individual homes. As our car pulled out of the unloading dock on the west side of the Records Building to enter Houston Street, for just an instant we were facing, not fifty yards away, the spot where on the 22nd of November 1963, this entire unbelievable episode of world history had first begun to unfold. In slightly less than four months, enough world-shaking history had been made to fill volumes of history books. The world would long remember the past four months. Argumentative speculation regarding the president's assassination, and the trial of Jack Ruby, the man who assassinated the accused assassin after he had been arrested and was in the custody of law enforcement officers, would go on forever.

There was much criticism about the speed of our deliberation and our verdict when once we did assemble at the jury deliberation table on that Saturday morning. In our defense, I wonder if those critics ever stopped to consider that we individually had more than twenty-four hours to ponder the last of the evidence we had heard? Remember that Dr. Gibbs had stepped down from the stand Friday morning, the day before. After Dr. Gibbs' testimony, we heard nothing new in the way of evidence, only emotion-packed pleas. Why then was it so surprising when we reached a decision in two and one-half hours? We had been commended by both the defense and the prosecution, during their final arguments, on our intelligence. Shouldn't intelligent jurors be able to weigh the factual evidence and reach a stable decision without first having to sit through five hours of emotional, persuasive debate? Emotional persuasiveness that challenged our respect for American justice, our interpretation of malice, our love for our president, our civic guilt, our respect for law, our compassionate scientific intellects, and our patriotic responsibilities. These were all very learned counselors with most eloquent talents, but nothing they could say during final arguments could alter the evidence we had heard over the past ten days.

Certainly, our interpretation of that evidence is now and always will be open to question. Perhaps twelve other jurors from other walks of life, whether they were from Dallas or Dalhart, might possibly have reached a different verdict, but to each of us, the defense counsel had completely failed to establish a reasonable doubt in our minds that Jack Ruby did not know right from wrong and the nature and consequences of his act at the time he shot Lee Harvey Oswald.

My trial as a juror did not end as I had expected it to, with the dismissal of the jury. When I reached my home that Saturday afternoon, I found out that my wife had received several menacing telephone calls within the first hour after the verdict was announced. One caller told her, "Your son-of-a-bitch husband should be shot right between the eyes." Another caller stated, "I hope that damn husband of yours gets whatever he deserves for that verdict." After the first few calls came in, one of our neighbor ladies started answering the phone, and as soon as she determined that it was a disturbance call, she would hang up the phone.

My wife had our suitcase packed, and we were walking out the front door within ten minutes after I had returned home. However, even this short delay had been long enough to allow TV newsmen to arrive at my house in hopes of a statement. In an effort to not be rude and still not grant an interview, I did agree to talk with the newsman who taped my comments on the way to the car. I gave him a simple statement to the effect that our verdict was the only one we could have reached based on the evidence as we saw it presented.

The Dallas Morning News published an article in its Sunday, March 15 edition detailing how reporters had gone to the residence of each juror seeking comment on the trial, but found most of the jurors away from home. The reporter did speak with the wife of juror James E. Cunningham, who told the reporter Cunningham had no comment on the trial, and added, "He won't even tell me about it." Incredibly, the *News* published the street address of every juror (Martin 1964, 16-A).

Public reaction in Dallas to the verdict was mostly positive, but not overwhelmingly so. The headline of an article in the *News* read, "Most Agree Verdict Just," but also carried the subhead, "Some Persons Feel Penalty Too Severe." A woman (occupation not given) responded, "Surprised at the verdict? I'm amazed, it was unreal. The way the district attorney put it, it was either life or death, and that's a pretty big margin. I think Ruby is a sick man. Dallas is prejudiced, but no one wants to admit it." A male attorney told the *News*, "I agree with the verdict. There was no question that the man [Ruby] was not insane. He was seeking publicity" (Conde 1964, 23-A).

I had intended to spend the weekend with my father and mother on their farm, located about forty miles northeast of Garland. However, my newly regained freedom was such a wonderful new experience that I couldn't resist the temptation of doing just as I pleased. So, after the late TV news, my wife and I decided that we would return to our home in Garland. We knew that with the hour it would take for us to drive the forty miles it would be nearing midnight and most likely be too late for newsmen who might still be seeking an interview.

As we walked in the door, our telephone was ringing but we didn't answer it. Without turning on any lights, we put the children to bed and then we retired. I was awakened about 6:30 A.M. by the telephone ringing and I made the mistake of answering it. There was what sounded like a hysterical, whining voice at the other end who said something like, "Lord, Lord, Lord, I guess you will be going to church again today, will you?" My only answer was, "Yes, I certainly intend to do just that and I hope you will also," and I slammed the receiver down.

We did go to church that Sunday morning as we had always done in the past. After church, we went out to lunch at one of the area cafeterias. It was a bit embarrassing for me that day and for several weeks that followed, because everywhere I went I would run into someone I didn't know who recognized me from my picture that had been run so many times during the three weeks I was on the jury. I actually found that many times when I'd start to offer identification required to cash a personal check, the clerk would quickly decline any additional identification and approve the check, saying, "Oh, I know who you are Mr. Causey. That will not be necessary."

I have been told by several newsmen that during the last week of February and the first two weeks of March 1964, my name and picture ran in more newspapers across the country than any other man during the same time. My picture and short resume had been released to the news media by my employer, LTV. The morning after my acceptance as a juror, my picture and the short resume appeared in every major newspaper in the United States and several foreign papers. One of the most ego-inflating instances that came from all this publicity was when I received a letter postmarked in Switzerland. It was addressed: Max E. Causey, Dallas, Texas, USA. This letter was delivered to my home address in Garland, without so much as a street address. The letter was written in German, which, of course, I could not read. I had it translated as best as the translator could distinguish the handwriting. After reading the translation, I wondered if I should have gone to the trouble. The letter disagreed bitterly with the verdict and further stated that if we would send Ruby to his country of Switzerland, they would give him a medal, make him a national hero, and he would become a living legend.

One of the many articles on the trial was published in a French magazine *Paris Match*. The article focused on juror Mildred McCollum, but contained a section on the Causeys. This passage was

translated by a relative: "Max Causey is 35-years-old. I [the article's author] watched his face at the moment when lawyer Melvin Belli announced that he was the first juror accepted by the defense. Nobody was expecting that, and Max Causey less than anyone. . . . In favor of Causey, there was a determining argument. This electronics expert . . . had a major concern in his life: His second son, Kevin, is a retarded child. . . . [The article said Ruby's defense team had discovered this while doing research on the prospective jurors.] Max and Rosemary Causey aren't ashamed of this child. On the contrary, they go out with him, talk often of him and have even explained to their eldest son that, later, he will have the responsibility of this young brother in his life.

"For five years, because of Kevin, Max Causey has studied mental problems. Now, for Melvin Belli, it is the mental state of Ruby at the moment of the assassination of Oswald, which is the crucial point in the trial.

"In the small courtroom, when Belli said 'accepted,' I saw Causey hide his head in his hands, then get up slowly. His nomination signified that for days perhaps weeks, as long as the trial lasted, he would be shut out from the outside world. Max Causey, henceforth, hadn't even the right to telephone his wife.

"Rosemary [Causey], a petite, pretty brunette with glasses, learned the news through the journalists. . . . 'He will be, I am sure,' she said, 'an excellent juror. However, I am sad. After ten years of marriage, we are still in love with each other as on the first day'" (Mathias 1964, 101–102).

I received a total of thirty-seven letters about evenly split in agreement and disagreement with the verdict. I found one letter extremely interesting. It came from Ecuador in South America. It was neatly typed and attached with it was a carbon copy of a letter that had been sent to Ruby. The letter appeared to be a form letter, and according to the letter addressed to Ruby, this was to be a copy of a carload of such letters scheduled to be distributed in the Dallas area. The letter bitterly attacked the verdict and stated that Judge Brown, Henry Wade and Max E. Causey deserved the punishment instead of Ruby. The last sentence of the letter carried a very familiar "red" ring to it. It read, "After all, didn't he [Ruby] do exactly what the USIS/CIA wanted?" I was much amused by this letter. It smelled strongly of the red line of the Communist world. This letter made me feel better, because if somewhere in this world an advocate of this line disagreed with the verdict, then it strengthened the verdict insofar as I was concerned.

Among the mail agreeing with the verdict was a Western Union wire from Roselle, Illinois. The wire represented 1,500 members of that community who agreed with our verdict. I did not appreciate one approving letter due to the reasons given thanking us for the verdict. This letter was so full of anti-Semitic hate that after reading it, I burned it. Now I'm sorry that I didn't keep it along with all the others. Along with the letter was a packet of filthy, vile, anti-Semitic propaganda literature. I wondered just how warped can a person's mind be to concur with this type of reasoning. While I didn't enjoy receiving those letters condemning the verdict, I liked even less this type of approval.

There were many good, and some poor, articles written regarding the Ruby trial and verdict. Many of the articles bitterly condemned the jury for such a hasty and harsh sentence. Some articles took the defense team to task for improper conduct of the defense. A vast number of the writers criticized Judge Brown for the laxness that they felt allowed "showmanship" to prevail throughout the trial. We all know that it's always easier to be a Monday morning quarterback than it is to prove your mettle on the turf on Sunday.

A disdainful editorial titled "The Shame of Dallas, Texas" appeared in the *Saturday Evening Post* following the trial. It spared no one: "The trial of Jack Ruby was another unbelievable event. At a time when every effort should have been exerted to secure as fair, as dignified and as decorous a trial as possible, publicity once again seemed to outweigh every other consideration. . . . On Saturday afternoon, March 14, as the nation watched on television, a circus atmosphere prevailed in the courtroom. When the verdict was announced, reporters and photographers climbed over benches and chairs. Ruby's showboat lawyer, Melvin Belli, displayed his lack of respect for the judicial process by blurting out that the court was a 'kangaroo court, a railroad court.' Who can forget Judge Joe B. Brown as he read the verdict . . . wetting his fingers and casually turning the pages of the decision as if it were a bill of lading, or some infinitely boring memorandum? . . . Now, unless the finding of the jury is upset, Jack Ruby will be dragged from his cell one day. He will be strapped into an electric chair. . . . Somehow, in a simple-minded way, through this barbaric anachronism, society will conclude that 'justice' has been done. What actually will have happened is that Jack Ruby, one of the lowest creatures in memory, will have dragged society down to his level" ("The Shame of Dallas" 1964, 82).

An article in *Time* that appeared after the verdict was reversed by the Texas Court of Criminal Appeals in 1966, referred to Judge Brown as "bumptious" ("Objection Sustained" 1966). The *Time* article written immediately after the verdict focused almost entirely on the testimony of the defense psychiatrists and ignored the evidence presented by the prosecution ("Death for Ruby" 1964, 27–28).

Before the ink dries on my last statement, I would like to try my hand at quarterbacking the Ruby defense, and state what I, and only I, feel should have been the defense's case. These opinions are my own and were not formed in collaboration with the other jurors.

I personally feel that Mr. Belli and his team selected a nearly impossible defense for Ruby. First of all, Ruby was by law legally sane until the defense could prove beyond a reasonable doubt, under the McNaughten Rule, that he was insane at the time he shot Oswald. Secondly, and understandable under the circumstances, the defense never denied that Ruby shot Oswald. Therefore, the only defense offered on Ruby's behalf was that he was suffering from a psychomotor epileptic seizure at the time of the shooting that prevented his knowing the difference between right and wrong or the nature and consequences of his act. To me, this defense selected by Mr. Belli and his defense counsel proved to be very difficult to sell.

It was not literally so that Ruby's mental illness had to be proved "beyond a reasonable doubt," according to Judge Brown's charge to the jury, but clearly the jury was justified in requiring a firm standard of proof. Based on Causey's preceding statement, it appears this part of the charge was very influential: "Every person charged with an offense is presumed to be sane . . . until the contrary is shown by proof. If . . . the guilt of the defendant has been established beyond a reasonable doubt, it devolves on the defendant to establish his insanity at the time of committing the act in order to excuse himself from legal responsibility." The following part of Judge Brown's charge may not have resonated as strongly with the jury: "It is not necessary that the insanity of the defendant should be established beyond a reasonable doubt." But the judge went on to tell the jury: "It is sufficient if it be established to your satisfaction by the weight or preponderance of the evidence. . . ." (Kaplan and Waltz 1965, 308–309)

From Causey's writing and from interviews with jurors Flechtner, Holton, Rose and Sowell, it is clear they believed Ruby's mental illness was not strongly established. The jurors tightly focused on the question of whether Ruby knew right from wrong and had control of his actions when he killed Oswald, under the McNaughten Rule, and as the defense psychiatrists could not or would not make definitive statements on this crucial issue, the jury remained unconvinced by their testimony.

In my layman's opinion, any good lawyer could have gotten Ruby off with something less than a death sentence if he had thrown Ruby on the mercy of the court and pleaded plain old "temporary insanity" brought on by emotional stress over the loss of his beloved president.

Ruby's emotional reaction to the assassination of President Kennedy was well-documented in the trial. For example, psychiatrist Dr. Manfred Guttmacher testified that, as a Jew, Ruby strongly identified with Kennedy because of his minority status as a Catholic and because of Kennedy's strong stand on civil rights. Guttmacher testified that Ruby used "terms such as 'I fell for that man [Kennedy],' the kind of terms which one uses really for someone that . . . one is in love with" (Statement of Facts, 1009).

With a defendant of less notoriety, I believe that a good defense counsel could possibly have drawn a verdict of ten years. In Ruby's case, he was reasonably well-known as a nightclub operator, and no doubt, this would have made the defense counsel's case tougher to make. Even so, he could have drawn perhaps ten to twenty years. I do not personally believe that any jury would have let Ruby off, regardless of the defense's plea, on a suspended sentence.

If I had been Mr. Belli, and had been convinced that I could win the case with psychomotor epileptic insanity, I would have paraded additional medical witnesses to the stand who would have been willing to testify that they had a positive opinion that Ruby did not know the difference between right and wrong and the nature and consequences of his act at the time he shot Oswald.

As it turned out, the defense counsel was numerically defeated in the medical experts willing to testify pertaining to an opinion on Ruby's sanity under the McNaughten Rule. [The prosecution presented eight medical witnesses to five for the defense.] Had the famous Dr. Gibbs ventured an opinion regarding Ruby's insanity, this would have weighed heavily in Ruby's favor, insofar as I was concerned. Mr. Belli had objected to Dr. Gibbs being asked his opinion on this question, and further stated that Dr. Gibbs was not qualified to answer such a question since he was only acquainted with the EEG tracings and had not been privileged to the complete medical findings. Perhaps, technically, Mr. Belli was right, but if so, how could twelve medically unqualified jurors be asked to reach such an opinion? If Dr. Gibbs was not qualified to offer such an opinion, for whatever weight it might carry, then certainly neither were we. So, therefore, failure to have an opinion as to the sanity of a man leaves his condition status quo or sane. We the jury felt that Ruby was sane.

Section III

Voir Dire

Excerpts of the questioning of
Max Causey by the defense

Editor's Note: The defense was not ready to accept the idea that Judge Joe Brown would allow television viewers who saw the shooting of Lee Harvey Oswald to serve as jurors. Melvin Belli and his team wanted all television viewers of the crime to be declared as witnesses, which would disqualify them as jurors under Texas law. The prosecution was equally determined that television viewers be allowed to serve. Causey had testified that he had seen a television replay of the shooting.

On Feb. 20, 1964, following a routine examination by District Attorney Henry Wade lasting about twenty minutes, and a recess for lunch, Max Causey was questioned by defense attorney Melvin Belli. The famed lawyer posed several questions in which he suggested to Causey that he could be facing a lengthy time of service as a juror: up to ten more days for jury selection, several weeks for the trial itself, and two to three weeks of jury deliberations. The prosecution objected to all of these questions, and the Court sustained the objections. Judge Brown then intoned, "Let's get down to qualifying of the juror." The following are excerpts from Belli's questioning of Causey, transcribed from the trial. Again, editorial insertions are in brackets or boldface.

Belli: Now, will you tell us what you remember, what you saw on video, the shooting?

Causey: Well, about the only thing that I can recall was that I saw a person's back, it seemed to jump or hurdle some obstruction, some restriction.

Belli: Well, I put it to you, sir, and ask you if it wasn't true, this man didn't hurdle or jump, that this man . . .

[Prosecution attorney] Jim Bowie: To which we object.

Judge Brown: Sustain the objection to it.

Belli: Your Honor, I think that this pointed up precisely that as a witness, I would have to cross-examine him, because that's not what we intend to prove, that a man hurdled or went ahead so abruptly to shoot someone else. [To Causey] Do you believe that someone hurdled something to shoot someone else?

Bowie: To which we object, Your Honor. This is no test for the qualifying of a juror.

Judge Brown: All right.

Belli: No, it isn't. It's the disqualification of a witness.

Bowie: To which we object, Your Honor. The gentleman is not a witness in any shape, form or fashion.

Judge Brown: Sustain the objection. . . .

Belli: Will you tell us what you saw?

Causey: As I recall, I saw a person's back, [he] seemed to take hurried or excited steps forward. And I never saw the face. I only saw the back; I never heard a shot. Mr. Oswald slumped to the floor.

Belli: . . . Who was it that you saw come forward?

Causey: I couldn't say, sir.

Belli: Do you have an opinion at the present time who it was?

Causey: No, sir.

Belli: Of all the people in Dallas, you wouldn't think that it was more likely to be one person than another, is that right?

Bowie: Objection.

Judge Brown: Sustained.

Belli: . . . As you sit there now, you don't have an opinion it was Jack Ruby who came forward, is that right?

[District Attorney] Henry Wade: This is repetitious, Your Honor.

Judge Brown: Sustained.

Belli: And you did read subsequently that it was Jack Ruby who came forward?

Causey: Yes, sir.

Belli: . . . And you heard someone say something like, "Jack, you son of a bitch, get away from here," something like that, didn't you?

Causey: No sir, I never heard that. I read it. I read that at a later date somewhere, but I don't recall hearing that on TV at the time.

Belli: Do you know who was supposed to have said that?

Causey: No, sir.

Belli: Did you hear the shot?

Causey: No, sir.

Belli: Did you see any smoke?

Causey: No, sir.

Belli: Did you see anybody wrestling or wrestled to the floor?

Causey: I couldn't definitely say. I saw Mr. Oswald slump to the floor and there was commotion. I couldn't say for certain.

Belli: Did you note that the man who shot Mr. Oswald had a gun in his hand?

Causey: I couldn't tell that, sir.

Belli: Did you see a gun at all?

Causey: No, sir.

Belli: Did you see the video from the beginning to the end?

Causey: I think so, sir.

Belli: How many feet did this person go between the time that you first saw him come into view, and the time that he stopped—five feet?

Causey: I would say more than that—ten.

Belli: Ten feet—is that right?

Causey: That's a good guess, yes, sir.

Belli: And if I were to cross-examine or examine other witnesses to show that he only went three feet, you still have a recollection and opinion that he went about ten feet, wouldn't you?

Bowie: Objection.

Judge Brown: Sustain the objection.

Belli: Do you think that with the production of evidence on the part of the defense, that I could erase from your mind the opinion that he went ten feet or would that be difficult?

Causey: It would be difficult.

Belli: It would be what?

[Defense attorney] Joe Tonahill: He said, "It would be difficult."

Belli: I believe Mr. Tonahill, but the witness is under oath, so we would like to have it in the record, Your Honor, if we may. Do we have it, "I believe it would be difficult"?

Bowie: We object to that, Your Honor, to ask this witness to make an estimate that he had guessed at and then go and say, "Now, you formed an opinion about this estimate." And so this is a very highly improper question.

Judge Brown: Sustain the objection . . .

After more sparring over the propriety of the questions being asked of Causey, and more questioning in a similar vein by Belli, the defense attorney said, "We challenge for cause," meaning that the defense was ready to reject Causey as a juror. At this point, Judge Brown asked Belli, "Do you mind if I ask him a question?" Belli replied, "Well, if I said no, Your Honor, I am afraid I would be in trouble. So I will tell Your Honor, yes, to go ahead."

Judge Brown: Are these opinions that you have such that you could set aside, if you were selected to serve on the jury, and give the defendant a fair and impartial trial?

Causey: Well, sir, the prosecution would have to prove to me that it was Mr. Ruby.

Judge Brown: What I want to know, the opinions that Mr. Belli has asked you about, are they so fixed or are they such that you could not lay them aside and go into the jury box as a fair and impartial juror?

Causey: I think I could set them aside, sir.

Judge Brown: Well, now, could you or would you; can you or can't you?

Causey: I can.

Judge Brown: All right.

Belli: It would take evidence to remove those opinions, right?

Bowie: We object, Your Honor, the court has asked those questions.

Judge Brown: Sustain the objection.

Tonahill: Judge, if it would take evidence to remove the opinion, then this gentleman certainly is disqualified because he would keep them.

Judge Brown: He just answered the question, counsel.

Tonahill: He answered a conclusion, which means nothing. But if he says it would take evidence to remove the opinion, then it's a fixed opinion.

Judge Brown: Let me ask another question. Do these opinions, do they lead to your opinion as to his guilt or innocence, these opinions you have just expressed?

Causey: You mean Mr. Ruby?

Judge Brown: Yes, sir.

Causey: No, sir.

Judge Brown: All right. I am going to hold that he is qualified, gentlemen, so far.

Belli: Do you feel that there is any question of your city being on trial here along with Jack Ruby?

Mr. Causey: No, sir. I live in Garland. [Laughter]

Judge Brown: Sheriff, if there is any more laughter, I want the people who laugh removed from the courtroom.

Sheriff Bill Decker: All right, Judge.

Belli: Living in Garland is still a part of Dallas, is it not?

Causey: It's part of Dallas County, sir.

Belli: Is there anything you have seen in various magazines or newspapers that [refer to] and I put it in context, "the shame of Dallas"?

Causey: No, sir. I haven't seen anything that makes me feel like my city is on trial, if that's the question you ask.

Belli's questioning, becoming noticeably less contentious, then moved on to Causey's emotions and feelings regarding the assassination of President Kennedy and the killing of Oswald. Finally, Judge Brown directed Mr. Belli to "move on," at which point Belli began to question Mr. Causey on his feeling toward insanity.

Belli: Let's go further into the emotional area. You do appreciate that a man acts rationally, by intelligence, and also by emotion. Right?

Causey: Yes, sir.

Belli: And we approach two areas here, we approach the area that the man who shot Mr. Oswald was in . . . that he might have been activated intelligently or he might have been activated by a diseased mind. Do you think that is possible?

Causey: Definitely.

Belli: On the issue of insanity, did you have any educational experience or otherwise, in the field of psychology, as distinguished from psychiatry?

Causey: I have a master's degree in education.

Belli: Well, with a master's degree in education, you appreciate that psychiatry and psychology are distinct. Right?

Causey: Yes, sir.

Belli: Now, would you wait until you have heard all of the evidence here from all of the psychiatrists, their standing in their own profession, their standing in their community, before you make up your mind as to the mental cerebration, or activities more or less of Mr. Ruby, if you are chosen as a juror?

Causey: Definitely.

Belli: Do you have any opinion on the question of the state of insanity, for a short period of time, or for varying periods of time?

Bowie: To which we object, Your Honor.

Judge Brown: Did you say, do you have any opinion?

Belli: That's right.

Judge Brown: All right.

Belli: Subject to all these questions, Your Honor. [To Causey] That last question, can you answer?

Causey: Would you ask the question again?

Belli: Withdraw . . .

Belli: How about the business or occupation, whatever you want to call it, that Mr. Ruby was in? He was running, I think, what we call a striptease joint here in Dallas. Is there anything that imposes any impediment or problem to you, and to your candid deliberation, if chosen as a juror, because of his occupation?

Causey: No, sir.

Belli: This question of whether he had any connections with Oswald,

I think we have gone through that, that there was . . . that doesn't cause any impediment, does it; you wouldn't believe any of that stuff you read in the paper?

Bowie: We object to that, Your Honor.

Judge Brown: Sustain the objection.

After other questioning concerning Causey's opinion on the McNaughten Rule, his familiarity with the names of some of the psychiatrists who would testify in the trial, and other assorted topics, Belli's assistant, Joe Tonahill, finally told Judge Brown, "We pass him [back to the State]." Wade then said, "Mr. Causey, the State will accept you on the jury."

Belli still wasn't quite ready to accept Causey as the first juror:

Belli: I want to know if we're going to have extra challenges, if Your Honor please? And we would like to know before . . .

Judge Brown: I can't tell you that at this time, Mr. Belli.

Belli: You see, we don't know, I would ordinarily accept this juror, but we have a problem of . . .

Wade: Judge, we object to any of this.

Judge Brown: The Court will sustain the objection. Mr. Belli, either accept him or reject him.

Belli: Your Honor will not tell us at this time whether you are going to give us extra challenges?

Judge Brown: No, sir, I can't tell you at this time, Mr. Belli. The thought never entered my mind.

Belli: We renew our motion for a change of venue at this time on the Court's own motion.

Judge Brown: The Court overrules your motion.

Belli: We accept this juror.

Judge Brown: All right. Mr. Causey, would you raise your right hand, please sir, and be sworn? (Statement of Facts, 637–684)

HENRY WADE
DISTRICT ATTORNEY
RECORDS BUILDING
DALLAS, TEXAS 75202

March 19, 1964

Mr. Max E. Causey
710 Peachtree Lane
Garland, Texas

Dear Mr. Causey:

Kindly accept this letter as my personal thanks for your jury service in the Jack Ruby case. It is realized that your jury service created many hardships upon yourself and family but it should be stated that regardless of such matters you met a very great responsibility with courage and intelligence. For this I am deeply thankful.

Your verdict is most outstanding because it will deter others from so wantonly taking human life without due process of law. The framers of our Constitution provided for trials by jury because of their unquestioned faith that the American citizen would follow the law and **Letters** enforcement. Your verdict has again proven the correctness of the jury system and has given renewed faith in the American citizen as a person who will meet the responsibilities of such citizenship.

Again let me thank you for your verdict and service as a juror. For such I shall ever be grateful.

Sincerely yours,

HENRY WADE
Criminal District Attorney
Dallas County, Texas

HW:sc

Editor's Note: One of the remarkable things about the Causey family's experience is the publicity they received as a result of Max serving as foreman of the Ruby trial jury. When Causey was chosen as the first juror, the news appeared on the front page of both Dallas daily newspapers. Feature articles on the family, containing their Garland address, followed. Walter Cronkite's *CBS Evening News* produced a feature on the Causey family. Other jurors and their families also received publicity much greater than any that would be given to jurors in a high-profile trial today. But the Causeys received more than their share. And so, when the trial ended, they were the target of telephone calls and letters, some in support of the verdict and the sentence, some bitterly opposed. A selection of those letters is reproduced here. As in other sections of this book, they are presented with a minimum of editing. Names have been changed to initials to preserve anonymity. The letters give a sense of the passionate feelings regarding the trial of Jack Ruby, which occurred so soon after the John F. Kennedy assassination, and which was so closely associated with Dallas.

Dear Mr. Causey,

I can't imagine how twelve supposedly patriotic Americans can want to execute a fellow-American who has shot a Communist, who murdered our President on our Dallas streets.

The horrible create [sic] who shot our president, killed a Dallas policeman, and almost killed our Governor did not deserve to live. Although Oswald should have been tried and convicted by a jury, I still can understand Ruby's moment of misjudged patriotism. The state failed to prove their case against Ruby—for they did not prove motive, which it is necessary to do. In other words, they did not prove that Ruby killed him "to get fame and fortune."

The electric chair is a long way from justice in this case, and I hope someone on that jury will become a "Profile in Courage" and step out for a much lesser sentence for this poor, misguided little man. Have you already forgotten how you felt on Nov. 22, 1963? I haven't.

Sincerely yours,

Mrs. E. G.

Dallas, Texas

— ✖ —

3-14-64

Dear Mr. Causey,

Thank you for doing a hard job, well. You have restored my girls' faith in justice. God will continue to guide you.

Sincerely,

B. D.

— ✖ —

[From a Western Union Telegram]

Max Causey and jury members, care Dist. Atty. Wade Courthouse Dallas
Speaking for 1500 members of this community,

Congratulations to you and members of the jury for your forthright verdict. It was a most outstanding victory for law and order. Sorry we had no record of the jurors' names. Will gladly wire each juror on receipt of name.

F. M.

Roselee, Ill.

[Mr. Causey,]

Did you ever hear of the Jack Ruby trial? Well I am sorry to call it to your attention for it must be a sore spot in your heart by now and I might add, due entirely to your own lack of understanding of your duty plus carelessness. If ever there was a miscarriage of justice it was in the decision handed in by the jury in Dallas. Judge Brown himself could not have done worse as indicated by his conduct in the case, even though he would like to have done so.

In fact all the jury did was listen to a hi-fi and the judge's overruling of testimony. The verdict as rendered by the jury was merely an echo of the judge's feeling and clearly showed the spirit of Texas. The jurors had no mind of their own or any opinion based on the evidence presented. I could enter into a long name-calling contest here which would be appropriate but I assume you have already received many new titles, so the question remains, does Dallas like to see our Presidents murdered?

H. R. M.

———✖———

Max,

As a history "buff," I wanted to direct your attention to something you have probably realized already. One hundred years from now, history students will be analyzing "cause and effect" of the JFK assassination and your name will be quoted from the history books—and for centuries thereafter.

It is very rare indeed when the "average man" gets his name in history. (Law students will analyze the reason for your choice as juryman and foreman.) That will be quite a memorial to your name when you realize that millions of us will have the maximum of a grave marker as our personal history.

Maybe I'm a "nut" as well as a "buff," but it is something to be very proud of. You did make "your mark" in the span of this world and it must be quite a thrill to know that your name will be discussed over the centuries.

J. F.

———✖———

Congratulations,

Your jury acted intelligently, whatever they all say. You were not brainwashed with lies (a la Kruschev) by Mr. M. Belli. Your jury, men and women, acted fairly.

M. F.
Bronx, NY

———— ✖ ————

Mr. Joe E. Brown
Attorney at Law & Judge of Ruby's prosecution
Dallas, Texas
U.S.A.
March 16, 1964
Your honor:

You gave Jack Ruby the chair. Your honor, this verdict should be definite, but not for Ruby. Those who rightly deserve it are Henry Wade, Max E. Causey, Dallas Police, Dallas Politicians and yourself, your honor. For at the time of Kennedy's slaughtering you along with millions of Americans were potential killers, this being definitely proved by the fact that Lee Harvey Oswald was never given proper protection. And although you were the ones supposed to protect his life, you did nothing positive, thus approving of Lee's execution, and actually enforcing old-times [sic] Texas law.

In lieu of protection, he was abandoned to his fate in a wolves' world which extended throughout the world. You purposefully offered him to anyone mad enough to replace the firing squad by broadcasting and showing the exact time and place where he was to appear, signing his death certificate by falsely protecting him with a police detail limited enough to permit the passing of any prospect to carry out the understood orders.

Things were so carefully planned that even the vehicle for his transportation was not at the usual parking place, but a considerable distance. As you Dallas people claim, you have been disgraced; yes, but by yourselves, not by Ruby. Now you appear as proud best administers of justice, trying to keep appearances before the world by killing an innocent victim, when in fact you should be ashamed of such an action.

You may rightly state that this is none of my business, but the fact that I, like many other people in the world, could willingly have acted as executioner of Lee Harvey Oswald on the spot, bestows me the right to speak and believe that Lee had already declared through shots of "Pentothal." And that you found it a necessity to shut his mouth for good to avoid the possibility of a war with Russia, hence the reason of your looking for a Ruby to screen your dirty job, for you pushed him and you know it.

As for Melvin Belli, along with his battery of counselors, I just can't realize how in the world he ever got to be an outstanding lawyer. Looks as if he was bribed and is only putting in an act, for he precisely chose the least defensible angle for a fruitful defense. Your honor, you will please excuse the rudeness of this letter, but it may be good for Dallas people to know what other people think.

Under the circumstance, if you wish to regain your indisputable fame of "Champions of Justice and Good Will," and for the sake of justice and North America, you must set Ruby free on the double and declare him no more "CULPABLE" than you are.

After all didn't he do exactly what USIS/CIA wanted?

Respectfully yours,

F. E. P.

Guayaquil (Ecuador) S.A.

———✖——

Dallas

March 16

Dear Mr. Causey,

Congratulations on the sensible verdict which you and the other eleven on the jury rendered. It is most encouraging to see that there are some Dallas County residents who are not intimidated by liberal-communist propaganda against the death penalty and liberal-communist screams about the so-called shame of Dallas. The latter, of course, is a manufactured product of the lefties of the press.

Your jury has done Dallas and this nation a great service by standing by your Christian-American principles. Such evidence of "spine" is an inspiration to patriots everywhere.

Sincerely,

A. M. R.

W. F. F.

J. G.

P.S. Please convey our sentiments to the other members of the jury.

—— ✖ ——

Mr. Max Causey

Garland, Texas

Dear Mr. Causey:

Well . . . the verdict is just what I expected from this town. I had thought that they were all wrong about Dallas—I have only lived here two years—but I am now convinced that Mr. Belli was quite correct in his accusations regarding this town. Although for Jack Ruby's sake, he shouldn't have said anything. In Dallas . . . to get justice you have to butter up the "wheels" . . . and Belli didn't!

Let us hope that in the name of God, Justice, decency, humanity, and pity that we don't really execute this foolish little person who no doubt thought he was doing what was expected of some Dallasite. As he said, "You guys can't do [it] . . . someone had to."

As for myself and family, I am selling my business here and returning to my home state. It is not quite as flourishing as Texas, but I will feel like I am back again in the U.S.A. God forgive you jurors. You, too, are caught up in this horrible tangle that has changed Dallas from a clean decent city to WHATEVER it has become under Bruce Alger, General Walker, and H. L. Hunt.

Sincerely yours,

R. H. G.

—— ✖ ——

March 14

Dear member or members [of the jury],

Can you honestly feel that your decision is more justified than Ruby's crime? Your means of retaliation for ridicule can only be called barbaric. Your omnipotence disgusts me.

Sincerely,

N. T.

March 16, 1964
Jury of the Jack Ruby Case
Dallas, Texas
Dear Ladies & Gentlemen,

In the light of seeming declination of moral and spiritual values in our nation, we commend you for your righteous judgment in the Jack Ruby case. We hope that you and others like you will continue to uphold the biblical standard of capital punishment where it is merited. May God continue to direct your decisions to withstand all pressures of paganism.
God bless you,
Mr. and Mrs. M. G. C.

———✖———

Dear Max:

Well I hear on the news bulletin that you have been chosen as the first eligible juror on Jack Ruby's trial. Just as fast as the names are released my letters will come through to you. Jack Ruby is not to be given the DEATH PENALTY.

Your letter is short but I expect you to read and re-read and re-read and re-read and re-read this page from the HOLY BIBLE I have sent to you. I have underlined a few verses I want you to give extra concentration on. Let the best minister in your town translate this section from Isaiah chapters 53, 54, 55, and the first verse of 56. [Editor's note: Among the verses from Isaiah underlined is Verse 6, Chapter 53: "All we like sheep have gone astray; we have turned every one to his own way; and the Lord hath laid on him the iniquity of us all."]

Love to you and all who are lucky enough to qualify as jurors,
J. L. S.
Baltimore, MD
P.S. This is the most important trial in the history of the world.

———✖———

May 2, 1964
Dear Max:

I wish to take this means of expressing sincere thanks for a job well done to you as foreman of the jury on the Ruby trial.

You have added honor to the Causey name, and you have rendered a great and just service to this nation. Congratulations to you and your family.

My oldest son Robert, who lives in California, told us of calling you recently while in Dallas and how impressed he was with you. Robert is an exceptional young man of thirty-six who is a research scientist for Lockheed Aircraft Missiles and Space Co.

Since every Causey in America stems from one of three brothers who came to this country about 200 years ago from Scotland and settled in Carolina, we are naturally bound to be cousins. The next time I get to Dallas I will make it a point to look you up. Would like to meet your family and have you meet some of mine.

With sincere personal regards and best wishes, I remain

Your cousin,

L.K. Causey, D.C., Ph.C.
Bowling Green, Ky.

———✖———

April 19, 1964
Max E. Causey
c/o Ling-Temco-Vought, Inc.
Dallas, Texas
Dear Sir:

Herewith is a memo relative to Capital Punishment reviewing Jesus the Christ's statements and personal attitude toward Capital Punishment and laws implementing that penalty.

You may care to take note of the memo.

[Editor's note: The following is an excerpt from the four-page, typed, single-spaced document.] "As a mature man Jesus dealt with the question of capital punishment and rendered His opinion during the supreme hours of His trial before Governor Pilate and the climactic minutes of His crucifixion.

"Taken prisoner and tried before the high tribunal of His country, Jesus was sentenced to death by crucifixion on a cross.

"Jesus submitted Himself to the jurisdiction of and penalty decreed by the court. In so doing He acknowledged the right of constituted judicial authority to take the life of a citizen when he had had his day in the court. (Copyright, 1963, S. J. Figley)"

Respectfully,

S. J. F.

Kansas City, Kan.

———— ✖ ————

[Editor's note: The following is excerpted from a three-page, typed, single-spaced document.]

March 18, 1964

[Addressed to all of the Ruby trial jurors]

Ladies and Gentlemen:

This letter is written not in the spirit of anger, dislike for you personally, or intolerance, but in a spirit of deep concern to see righteousness practiced in this as well as other lands.

Yes, practiced in the Spirit which Jesus Christ portrayed to the world, which is that of love and mercy: "Father have mercy on them for they know not what they do," and do unto others as you have them do unto you. I ask you, were you guilty of violating any of these precepts when you rendered the verdict of death in the Jack Ruby case? This is a time for deep soul-searching on your part. It is not something to be lightly tossed aside. . . .

One who has spark of the Spirit of Jesus within his own soul cannot fail to see in capital punishment anything less than legalized murder. It is merely a man-made law, devised out of fear and sanctioned out of ignorance, intolerance, hatred, anger, and such like negative qualities of the soul of man. You who sat on that jury were concerned with merely a man-made law which sanctioned the murder of a fellow being, to whom only God can give breath. . . .

Just two days ago I wrote my daughter that if she ever did such a thing as that jury (and others have done the same thing) did, if I had passed on, I would rise up from my grave and weep all the tears that had ever been shed in the world. . . . You judged Jack Ruby and you misjudged him, and now you are murdering him. . . . What a dastardly thing to be guilty of! Such fear itself is an evil thing.

Mrs. L. V. S.

— ✄ —

March 15, 1964

Mr. Max E. Causey,

You once stated to Mr. Belli, that you hadn't seen anything that made you feel your city was on trial. How true. I do believe that the whole nation felt that way. Nobody in their right mind could have blamed Dallas nor any Texas person for what Lee Harvey Oswald did. He did not belong to Texas. He was not Texas born. It was just unfortunate that he picked Dallas. Dallas was innocent that such a beast was among them. But, now, you and all that jury have brought shame and disgrace upon Dallas by your most unjust, unfair, unmerciful verdict. There were no true Christians among you. If Ruby goes to the electric chair, you too, all of you, should go with him. You should die for his life. And may the Almighty God strike you all and avenge Ruby.

An outrageous injustice that Ruby should have been sentenced to die for [killing] such an unworthy rat, beast, cruel, cold-hearted, bloody murderer. He [Oswald] committed many crimes. Ruby only accidentally committed one crime. He acted on an impulse. He felt too strongly in his mind what the whole nation felt, and some unnamable force of justice to avenge the death of two good men caused Ruby to act as he did. He was chosen to do what millions of people wanted to do on that day. Ruby should have been given a medal, my husband has always said.

None of you understand human nature! Your cruel judgment tops all of the cruel killings that Lee Harvey Oswald did. Now you, not him, have shamed Dallas. Send this letter to others of the jury and let them see how the world feels about this unfair trial and unfair jury. His mother, Lee Harvey Oswald's, is right. She should be granted her wish, that Ruby live. Lee Harvey Oswald was not worthy of a man's life. How could you give a verdict of guilty?

Mr. and Mrs. D.

Brooklyn, NY

Mar. 16, 1964

Dear Mr. Causey:

Congratulations on your fair, square verdict on the Ruby trial. We have three boys sixteen, eighteen, twenty-one, and they see and read of the "hoods" getting off "scot-free"—too many times. We can use much of your justice up here.

Sincerely,

J. W. H.

Springfield, Ill.

———✖———

6/17/64

Dear Mr. Causey,

Last April I mailed you a photograph of that jury who did their duty in such a quiet way when you, as their foreman, brought in the unanimous verdict of guilty. It was the only thing the jury could do and they did not shirk that duty.

I bought the photograph showing the jury in the jury box. With it I enclosed my personal check to cover return postage with the hope that you would sign it for me with your name. I mailed it to the District Attorney's office, as I did not have your address. The prosecuting district attorney signed his photograph that I had mailed him as did the presiding judge.

Very shortly before Pres. Kennedy's death, he presented me with his inscribed photograph thanking me for the signed photograph I had mailed him of the Japanese naval officer who had rammed the PT-109. I would like very much to have you sign that photograph because it was a jury that refused to be intimidated or bulldozed by appeals in bombastic oratory. I am a Republican and that jury made me proud.

Sincerely,

C. G.

Minister

———✖———

Atlantic City, New Jersey
February 21, 1964
Mr. Max E. Causey
c/o the Court-Room of the trial of Mr. Jack Ruby
Dallas, Texas
My most dear Mr. Causey,

I am a young lad eighteen years of age, and since birth, I have been afflicted with a very severe condition of cerebral palsy, from which my doctors who have been treating me say I shall never completely recover.

This fact had led me to become very morose at time, but I nevertheless do try to pull myself through my depression.

I wish you to know that you indeed would make me very happy if you could find it in your heart to please sign with your personally-written signature the enclosed newspaper.

Most humbly, I implore you to do this small favor for me.

God bless you. And please let me hear from you very soon.

Respectfully,

L. A.

———✖——

Hillsboro, West Virginia
Feb. 27th, 1964
My Dear Mrs. Causey,

I just finished reading an article about you and your family in my daily paper, and I just could not resist writing this letter because of the words that were in the article about your retarded child. And I am going to take the time to explain why all these things mean so much to me and why I am so interested not only in one child but all children. [The Causey's youngest child, Kevin, suffered from phenylketonuria (PKU).]

First let me tell you why I was so attracted to you . . . your statement, "I cannot tell you why, but a retarded child brings you closer to God, to yourself and to each other. We call him 'our little angel.' He's a great blessing, and his big brother Keith loves him just as much as we do."

Now Mrs. Causey to me no sweeter words could ever have been spoken. I think you and your husband must be real children of God, and the very best Christians. [The writer goes on to tell the story of her grandchild who was afflicted with epilepsy.]

Again I say God bless you and your husband as well as your precious little family.

Your newfound friend,

Mrs. R. J. H.

———✕———

March 16

Dear Mr. Causey,

As foreman of the jury for the recent trial, my husband and I realize the pressure which must surely be on you and your family. You and the other members of the jury have been placed in a position of being scrutinized by many. We all know this was not of your asking.

Be assured that the majority of people realize the responsibility this must have been. It is not easy to determine a man's life or death.

Due to the circumstances of the trial, we feel that the decision reached was correct. The evidence, as we have read, offered little choice. You, along with the rest of the jury, will be in our thoughts and prayers.

I'm sure in time you and your family will be able to resume a normal life. The laws of this nation are just and must be upheld with the dignity and responsibility which you displayed.

Sincerely,

Mr. and Mrs. R. G. R.

Section V

Selected Articles

Wife Says Mate To Be Good Juror

By HUGH AYNESWORTH

e wife of the first juror
ed for the Jack Ruby murder
said Thursday she didn't
him to serve on the jury but
he would be "a fair, good
r."

s. Rosemary Causey, 37, was
hing television with a long-
friend, Mrs. Frances Lock-
when the news flashed over
wire that her husband, Max,
ngineering planning specialist
Ling-Temco-Vought, had been
en.

just know he'll be gone a
time," she said as reporters,
ds and well-wishers began to
hone her. "I don't want him
e gone, but we realize it's
uty to serve."

second thought, the petite
ime physical education
er, added: "I think I'll send
Belli (defense attorney Mel-
Belli) a note telling him to
Max home . . . because I

Keith, missing a couple of front
teeth, explained that he loved
football and that he didn't particularly like his daddy being gone
for what is expected to be a
lengthy period.

He said he guessed his schoolmates would want to talk with
him about his father's role, but
added, "I don't care about that
. . . I just don't want him gone
very long."

studiously an-
swered many pointed questions to
pass the rigid test of an "impartial and fair" juror, didn't
want to be away from home
much, either.

"I am not interested in serving
on this jury," he told defense
attorneys.

He sat solidly in the witness
chair throughout the gruelling
questioning.

He wore a black suit, a red tie
and had a neat white handerchief
with his initials on it showing
slightly from his left suit pocket.
He appeared unmoved by all the

Editor's Note: As the first juror selected in the Jack Ruby trial, Max Causey received an enormous amount of publicity. These newspaper articles appeared in the days immediately following his selection as a juror and are re-printed here with the permission of the *Dallas Morning News.* Two of the articles were written by Jim Lehrer, who went on to fame as a public television news commentator and author, and Hugh Aynesworth, who is one of the most respected authors on the John F. Kennedy assassination.

All articles reprinted with the permission of *The Dallas Morning News*

"Juror Faces Lonely Life Until Joined by Another"

(Dallas Times Herald, Feb. 21, 1964)

By Jim Lehrer

Max E. Causey has taken 16 steps into a world where there are dominoes and playing cards, but no opponents—where there is much to say, but nobody to say it to.

Mr. Causey, the first juror accepted by both sides in the historic Jack Ruby murder trial, is now in virtual seclusion.

And he will remain that way until the second juror joins him. It could be awhile.

Unlocks door

After Judge Joe B. Brown swore the Garland man into jury service Thursday afternoon, court bailiff Bo Marbra unlocked a door behind the judge's bench.

The door opened to the [16] steps up to the jury deliberation room. Mr. Causey passed through the door and Mr. Mabra followed.

In the room at the top of those stairs the Ling-Temco-Vought electronics man will spend his days—alone. At night, he will sleep upstairs in the special jury quarters.

The only companion Mr. Causey will have will be Mr. Mabra, who, fortunately for the juror, is a warm, friendly man with a likable personality.

But Mr. Mabra will only be around for conversation at meal times and just before both men go to sleep at night.

Other duties

The rest of the time, the bailiff will be in the courtroom carrying out the other duties for the court and judge. In his pocket will be the key to the door behind which Mr. Causey is lodged.

The deliberation room, a half-floor up and behind the courtroom on the second floor of the Criminal Courts Building, is anything but spacious—22 by 12 feet, to be exact.

In the middle is a long table with 12 chairs around it and against one wall are a sofa and two stuffed chairs.

Off to one end is an even smaller room—12 feet by 12 feet—where there are tables for playing games. Domino sets and cards are available. Maybe Mr. Causey plays solitaire.

If Mr. Causey wants to see the outside world from his locked room, he may go over to the east wall to the windows. The view, however, is not the choicest. He will see only the two-yard breezeway between the Criminal Courts Building and the Records Building next door. Its main inhabitants are pigeons.

Allowed to read

Mr. Causey probably will be allowed to read, but only on matters that have nothing to do with the Ruby case or anything remotely connected with it.

The only times he will see outside people—until the second juror joins him—will be those three times a day he goes out for something to eat.

Bailiff Mabra usually takes locked-up jurors out to a nearby restaurant for all meals, rather than having them sent up from the Dallas County jail kitchen.

Unless there is a special change for the Ruby case, this is expected to be the practice for Mr. Causey.

At night, the 35-year-old juror will follow the bailiff to the jury quarters on Floor 7-M in the courts building. Mr. Causey will take one of the 14 small, clean bedrooms, furnished with a Hollywood bed and a lavatory.

The beds have pink bedspreads. The walls of the room are green.

Close by

Mr. Mabra will have a bedroom close by.

If Mr. Causey wants to send messages to his wife or business associates, he will have to do it through the bailiff. Mr. Mabra will have to tell Mrs. Causey, for instance, how many pairs of socks, shirts and other clothes her husband will need—to begin with.

It will be Mr. Mabra also who will arrange for the delivering and picking up of Mr. Causey's personal effects, including other items he will need to live away from home for awhile—razor, toothbrush, etc.

A lonely life is in the offing for Max E. Causey. And how does he feel about it all?

He won't be able to answer this or any other question until he and 11 other persons answer the more vital question of the guilt or innocence of Jack Ruby.

"Wife Says Mate To Be Good Juror"
(*Dallas Morning News*, Feb. 21, 1964)
By Hugh Aynesworth

The wife of the first juror picked for the Jack Ruby murder case said Thursday she didn't want him to serve on the jury but felt he would be "a fair, good juror."

Mrs. Rosemary Causey, 37, was watching television with a long-time friend, Mrs. Frances Locklear, when the news flashed over the wire that her husband, Max, an engineering planning specialist with Ling-Temco-Vought, had been chosen.

"I just know he'll be gone a long time," she said as reporters, friends and well-wishers began to telephone her. "I don't want him to be gone, but we realize it's his duty to serve."

On second thought, the petite one-time physical education teacher, added: "I think I'll send Mr. Belli (defense attorney Melvin Belli) a note telling him to send Max home . . . because I need him."

Both the Causeys have masters degrees, he in education and she in physical education. They both went to East Texas State College in Commerce.

Causey, 35, grew up at Caddo Mills and attended high school at Josephine. Rosemary went to Commerce High and later taught at Greenville High, where she was employed when they were wed in 1953.

Rosemary was thrilled to learn that she could exchange notes with Max. She was told, also, that these notes would be read by a bailiff before they were delivered—both ways.

"Oh well," she smiled with a twinkle in her eye, "I'm sure the bailiff's been in love."

The Causeys have two sons, Keith, 8, and Kevin, 5.

Keith, missing a couple of front teeth, explained that he loved football and that he didn't particularly like his daddy being gone for what is expected to be a lengthy period.

He said he guessed his schoolmates would want to talk with him about his father's role, but added, "I don't care about that . . . I just don't want him gone very long."

Causey, who studiously answered many pointed questions to pass the rigid test of an "impartial and fair" juror, didn't want to be away from home much, either.

"I am not interested in serving on this jury," he told defense attorneys.

He sat solidly in the witness chair throughout the grueling questioning.

He wore a black suit, a red tie and had a neat white handkerchief with his initials on it showing slightly from his left suit pocket. He appeared unmoved by all the bickering between state and prosecution attorneys, which took about a third of the time he was on the stand.

Only near the end—as defense attorneys gathered in a tightly knit conference in front of Ruby—did he seem to be nervous. He began to adjust and finger his tie.

His wife said they had discussed his being called for jury duty. She said he told her, "I'll bet it's for this Ruby thing."

"We discussed it a good bit," said Mrs. Causey, "and he said he thought he could be a good juror, if chosen."

And, apparently, the defense attorneys thought so, too. Belli, chief defense lawyer, said, "He's the kind we're looking for . . . intelligent, unemotional." Belli's aide, Joe Tonahill, offered to let Causey go home for the night, but Judge Joe B. Brown cut that short with the demand that the juror be sent to the dormitory upstairs from the courtroom—where he will remain.

Mrs. Causey said Max's parents, Corvie and Fannie Causey of Caddo Mills, "are sure going to be surprised. They don't have a television set. I'll bet they get one now."

He has a sister, too, Mrs. Jo Heath of Dallas.

The Causeys live in Garland, close to the LTV plant where Max has worked for eight years.

"We're usually homebodys," said Mrs. Causey. "I guess we'll really be now."

"Family Misses Juror"
(*Dallas Times Herald*, February 1964)
By Constance Watson

Rosemary Causey knew her husband would be on the stand Thursday and had listened to her transistor radio all day.

Then a member of the press telephoned and excitedly said her husband had been accepted as the first juror in the trial of Jack Ruby—the accused murderer of Lee Harvey Oswald.

"That's when all my work stopped," the petite brunette told the *Dallas Times Herald*. "I didn't believe they would agree on anyone, and then they chose my husband."

"I admit the first thing I said was 'Oh, no!' But then I don't think any wife would want her husband to be gone from home for so long."

Late that afternoon at the Causey home, the telephone and doorbell still rang persistently. An ex-neighbor, Frances Locklear, took the calls while Rosemary described her husband, the first man Melvin Belli found acceptable to judge the fate of his client.

Max Causey, a 35-year-old planning specialist for Ling-Temco-Vought, is 5 feet 10 inches tall, stocky, blonde, blue eyed, a Baptist and a Democrat.

He moved his family to Dallas in 1956, the year he joined the electronics firm. He graduated from East Texas State College where he also received his master's degree in education, and he is an ex-Air Force pilot. Max Causey didn't see any action, and he works on government contracts at Ling-Temco-Vought.

"Although I didn't want him to serve, I said all along he would be a good juror. He can do it if anyone can," noted Mrs. Causey.

"He has absolutely no opinions on the case. He is fair and always very thoughtful."

He has never served on a jury before. Rosemary opened the mail about two weeks ago to find the jury summons and called her husband at work.

"He was very calm, he just said, 'I'll bet it's the Ruby case.'"

"Of course, we discussed some things beforehand," she said. "I remember Max talking about his feelings on capital punishment. He told me he would like to see it abolished, but as long as it is the law he believes in abiding by it."

Concerning Jack Ruby's gaudy defender, Melvin Belli, Mrs. Causey said, "He doesn't feel any resentment toward him. He admires both Belli and [prosecutor Henry] Wade."

"Max is such a calm person; I wish he were here now." She explains that Max is a great help to her especially with Kevin.

While eight-year-old Cary Keith (called Keith) stood nearby, she talked of their second son, five-year-old Kevin, who is a victim of PKU. He was diagnosed a victim of the disease, which causes mental retardation, when he was 20 months old.

"Max calls him a blessing to our family," she said slowly. "We call him our joy boy, or our angel. No one who hasn't been through this would understand the good he has done for us."

Both Rosemary and Max are members of the First Baptist Church in Garland. Because of Kevin, Rosemary goes to the church first and teaches Sunday school. When she comes home, Max takes Keith to church with him.

Before moving to their attractive Early American brick home almost a year ago, they had lived in a two bedroom frame on Lewis Drive in Garland. The third bedroom is kept for Max's grandmother, Mrs. Mary Cantrell of Caddo Mills, who is there now helping Rosemary.

"Max told me that if he were chosen, he felt it would be a three or four month deal. I really didn't want him to be chosen, but I understand his feeling that this is his civic responsibility."

She looked out the window, laughed a little and said, "I think I will send Belli a little message and tell him to hurry and let my husband come home. . . . I wonder how Max is feeling now?"

Section VI

Juror Interviews

J. Waymon Rose
Douglas Sowell
Robert "Bob" Flechtner
Glenn Holton

Editor's Note: Four Ruby trial jurors were interviewed for this book: J. Waymon Rose, Douglas Sowell, Robert "Bob" Flechtner, and Glenn Holton. Rose spoke with the editor in March 2000, and Sowell, Flechtner, and Holton were interviewed on three separate occasions beginning in the summer of 1998. The interviews are printed here virtually verbatim, with notes added from trial transcripts, newspaper articles, books, and other sources. More than thirty-five years have passed since the trial, and the former jurors were not able to refer to the trial records as they were being interviewed. Therefore, in some cases their memories of the trial do not precisely match each of the facts presented elsewhere in this book. In most of those cases, the mistake is not crucial and their words are allowed to stand without correction by the editor.

J. Waymon Rose

J. Waymon Rose was the tenth juror selected for the Ruby trial. At the time of the trial, and until his retirement in 1997, Rose was a sales representative for a furniture manufacturer. He also served more than twenty years in the U.S. Naval Air Reserve after a stint as a Navy fighter pilot in World War II.

JMD: Tell me your general memories of the trial. What stands out to you?
WR: I looked on it really as a symposium for a class we were attending. In the various aircraft that I flew when I was in the Navy, we had a week or ten days of intensive ground school before transitioning into another airplane, and this was just another classroom to learn what we were there for. I was impressed with the efficiency of the State [prosecution] with how they prepared their case. They weren't there to prove that he [Ruby] had murdered Oswald; they were there to prove that he did it with intent, and malice aforethought, and all the other things. I was impressed with how they went about doing that. I thought they did a very good job. I don't say that Mr. Belli didn't do a good job on his end, but he was certainly fighting a difficult course.
JMD: When you were selected for the jury, what was your reaction?
WR: Well, I really thought, "Damn it"[chuckles]. I had gone in there determined that I was not going to be a part of that jury. I went in

there determined that I could be as smart as they were. By the testimony that I gave, I felt surely that this was going to be grounds for either one or both sides to dismiss me. For example, they asked, and I don't know if it was the State or Belli, if I believed a person could do an irrational act that was entirely against his whole being and be regretful, and I said, "Yes, I remember in the Cotton Bowl [1954], Alabama and Rice, when Tommy Lewis, the captain of the Alabama team, jumped up off the bench and tackled Dickie Maegle going down the sidelines. And he was sorry that he did it, but he still did it."

Belli wrote that he was impressed when Rose told this story. Rose told the story to illustrate that he understood how someone could get "carried away" (Belli 1964, 139).

WR: Then another question was asked about could a person take part in an event and not have any recall. And I mentioned, yes, that during the war there were instances in which pilots would go off a carrier on a mission, a very hazardous mission, and come back and not have any recall from the time they took off the carrier until the time they landed back aboard. Yes, I could understand how you could get into a traumatic event, and have it blocked out of your mind. These kind of things, I felt would display a knowledge of human interaction [such] that I might get off without any problems, but I no sooner got that said till Mr. Belli jumped up and said the defense would be proud to have this man as a juror.

JMD: You thought maybe the prosecution might not take you?

WR: Well, yes, and then Mr. Wade got up and said the State would be proud to have this man. So, the first thing I knew, I was being hustled out of there by two bailiffs and thrown into this den with the other nine people.

JMD: Belli also said in his book that he wished you had been the foreman of the jury.

WR: Yes he did.

JMD: Wonder why he said that?

WR: I don't know. But he said I was tall, dark, and handsome, and I wonder why he said that, too [chuckles].

"Rose was a tall, handsome man with dark hair receding from a high forehead, prominent cheekbones, a long flat nose, dark, direct eyes and an authoritative manner of speech," wrote Belli (1964, 139).

JMD: What were your impressions of some of the principle people in the trial, for instance, of Belli?

WR: I thought he was an extraordinary man. He was flamboyant, well-educated, and well-informed on what he was doing. Seemed like he had a lot of medical background, but I think, typically, an attorney of his stature certainly did a lot of research. So, he had people working for him, if he didn't know it [the psychiatric information pertinent to the case], who brought him stuff. Paralegals can do a lot of work for you. But I thought he was very well-informed, I thought he did a very good job, and I was really sorry to see him lose.

JMD: How so?

WR: Well, to go to such effort and to have it end up with mud in your face, in that he lost the decision, that's tough to see. I like winners, I like people who perform and go that extra mile. I like to see them rewarded some way.

JMD: So his flamboyance did not put you off?

WR: No, no. From my background as a salesman, I guess I empathized with him because you've got to have some flair and some flamboyance to get ahead in that business, too.

JMD: What about Henry Wade?

WR: Well, Henry Wade was very businesslike. He didn't fool around. He, as they say today, told it like it is. I had high regard for Henry Wade.

JMD: Judge Brown, do you have memories of him?

WR: Yeah, I remember the judge as being very down to earth, and a very homespun type. And he didn't give Mr. Belli a lot of slack. He wouldn't let him deviate from his course. So I think he ran the courtroom very well.

JMD: He was criticized to some extent for ruling too often in favor of the prosecution.

WR: I know it. That's what I say, he didn't give Belli a lot of slack. I guess he could foresee a long trial, and he didn't want it to get all strung out.

JMD: What are your memories of Max Causey as jury foreman?

WR: When it came time to deliberate and to elect a foreman, there was no dispute at all that Max was going to be the foreman because he'd been there the longest. I was certainly in favor of that.

JMD: During the trial, did he act in any kind of leadership role?

WR: No, none at all. In fact, I don't think anybody exercised any leadership role. We were sort of all in this together. I don't recall that anybody was trying to run the show.

JMD: As I read some of what Max wrote and also a newspaper article that quoted bailiff Bo Mabra, he [Mabra] said you kind of took the role of keeping the jurors loose.

WR: Well, I had a lot of jokes that I brought with me, you know, in my mind. I knew we were in a tight situation where we had no way to vent our feelings and we sort of had to live together. And in order to make conversation and keep everybody on some kind of [comfortable] footing, you know, it just seemed that it came out. I certainly didn't go in there determined to tell jokes, but, if you're standing around and here's twelve people looking at one another, what are you going to do? So you get up and do a tap dance, whatever it takes. So if it turned out that I was a jokester, that's the way it was. I'd like to think that I live by a footloose-type of code. I enjoy life. If you're not having fun, you might as well go home.

JMD: Most of what I read said that the jury was a pretty compatible group.

WR: Yeah, you know, I was a little apprehensive about having the women around twenty-four hours a day, but that turned out to be no problem. We finally got a television in there. Our reception wasn't very good, and we were limited to the programming we could have. But, beyond that, we played cards and I read. My diary, I did it on my knee in the bed every night. Because those little rooms we were in, certainly, you didn't have a window, had nothing else in there except a commode and a bed and a wash basin. Had a hook on the back of the door to hang your clothes on, and a bare light bulb hanging down. I mean, you were in jail, too. So if you retired to the bedroom, you had nothing else but sleep or else sit and write, so I'd sit up and write what happened that day.

JMD: Tell me the story about the offer you received from *Life* magazine.

WR: They telephoned me and asked if I would consider them using it for an article in *Life* magazine, and could they read it. They would transcribe the diary, and type it out, as long as I got the copy back. So when they finished with it and brought it back, they said they would like to buy it for $25,000 if I would complete it. I said it *is* completed. No, they wanted me to write how the deliberations went. And I told them, no, I wouldn't do that. We had promised one another that we would never divulge how the deliberations went or tell how each one of us voted, and I wouldn't do that.

JMD: Of course, the defense was based on this psychomotor epilepsy condition that Ruby supposedly had, and you all obviously did not buy that.

WR: We didn't buy that. I forget the term, but I think I made a reference in my diary, the type of epilepsy that Belli claimed Ruby had. [Testimony showed] he actually had another form of epilepsy that would not give him the excuse that would cause him to lose control of himself. . . .

JMD: Now this was from one of the defense psychiatrists?

WR: One of the defense psychiatrists, yeah.

JMD: So you thought there was some conflicting testimony, even among the defense psychiatrists?

WR: These so-called expert witnesses, yeah.

One such instance of conflict possibly was this exchange between assistant district attorney Bill Alexander and Dr. Manfred Guttmacher, a psychiatrist testifying for the defense. Dr. Guttmacher had testified that Ruby suffered from psychomotor epilepsy:

"I don't think we have data on which we can tell whether this man was in a psychomotor epileptic attack at the time [of the murder], but it could have occurred in a person of his makeup under that degree of stress, without being at that moment a psychomotor epileptic attack."

Alexander: All right. If he wasn't laboring under a psychomotor attack, what was he laboring under?

Dr. Guttmacher: Under a brief psychotic episode I think is best called episodic dyscontrol. (Statement of Facts, 1131)

JMD: I noticed the prosecution put eight psychiatrists on the stand and the defense sent five up just during the trial. Was it the sheer numbers?

WR: Well, until you said those numbers, I frankly didn't recall how many were there. And as we sit and talk, I don't recall who said what, but my impressions were that they [the defense psychiatrists] didn't do Ruby any good.

JMD: Max [Causey] writes about the final witness who testified [for the defense], Dr. Frederic Gibbs. Do you have any recollection of that particular psychiatrist?

WR: No, I just remember that he was there.

JMD: It was no particular one [of the psychiatrists who testified] who clinched it for you?

WR: No, it was just the accumulation of testimony. And I didn't pick and choose through it. In fact, I have a notation here [reads from his notes]: "Dr. Gibbs was on the stand this morning. He must be an expert in his field, as I know of his work on EEG [electroencephalograms] prior to the event. I thought, though, that he failed impressively. It seems he quit the American Electro-encephalogical Society two years after he himself founded it through a, quote, 'disagreement,' with its other members. [Assistant district attorney] Bill Alexander summed up my own thinking when he described Dr. Gibbs as a, quote, 'heretic,' quitting the society when he found the others disagreed with him."

Assistant district attorney Bill Alexander asked Dr. Gibbs if he had resigned from the American Electroencephalography Society over a difference of opinion with his colleagues, and Dr. Gibbs said that was correct. Alexander then asked, "And you consider yourself a heretic in this field, do you not, and have referred to yourself as such?" Dr. Gibbs replied, "Possibly. I'd rather use another word." Dr. Gibbs resigned in a disagreement over how the society was certifying electroencephalographers (Statement of Facts, 1663).

JMD: If you had been in charge of conducting the defense, how might you have done it differently?

WR: I would have pleaded . . . no contest and fallen on the mercy of the court. . . . It was pitiful. You know, the man [Ruby] sat there day in and day out, and he didn't have a chance. He never really had a chance. I wanted him to get up and say, "Hey, I'm sorry, I did the wrong thing, I made a mistake." But he never did that.

JMD: The idea was very prevalent at the time, and it's reflected in a lot of the letters that the Causeys got, that a lot of people felt that Ruby did what they wish they could have done, that he did it out of patriotism or what have you.

WR: But you still don't take [someone's] life in your own hands.

JMD: Oh, no, but some jurors have suggested that if Belli had presented it like that, it might have been more effective, that the man [Ruby] lost his head . . .

WR: Lost his cool. But, still, you keep coming back to the fact that he went in there [the police station] and had a gun on him, so there's not a lot you can say about someone like that. You know, [the Texas state prison at] Huntsville is full of people like that. And Huntsville's full of people that you and I could say, for the deed they're in there for, "They're crazy to do that. They should plead insanity." Well, then all those people ought to plead insanity as well. You've got to draw the line somewhere.

JMD: Why the death penalty as opposed to, say, life in prison?

WR: Well, I'm for the death penalty. I'm for it to deter serious crime. And I don't think it's used enough. I don't mean that we ought to go around killing everybody, but until our laws get some teeth into them it's [violent crime] going to continue. . . . Again, I don't like to fool around. I want to get on with the program.

JMD: There was criticism, of course, from Belli that the jury represented the business interests of Dallas—he called it the "oligarchy"— and that the jury tried to regain the good name of the city of Dallas.

WR: Well, that was the one disappointment that I had in Mr. Belli. As an example of opinion, when we were in the jury room and reached a decision, we agreed among ourselves that when the decision was read, we'd all look Jack Ruby in the eye. "Don't forget it"—it went around the table—"look him in the eye, look him in the eye." As we filed in, word was passed back through the line, "Don't forget, look him in the eye."

When the decision was read, I wasn't looking at everybody else, I was looking at him. That was the last thought we had as we walked through the door, and two minutes later, we're looking him in the eye, so nobody could forget in two or three minutes. During the trial there was a lady reporter there from England that *Life* magazine had hired to write the story about the trial. And she [wrote], "As the judge read the verdict, the jury hung their heads in shame." Now how blatant can you be? Why would she have done that? I canceled my *Life* magazine subscription and wrote a scorching letter, but of course, I never got any reply. But that was the worst [example] of bad reporting that I have ever seen. . . . It still incenses me to this very day. As far as giving the city of Dallas a good name or bad, I don't think it had a thing to do with it [the jury's decision]. I thought we were seeking justice. That's what I was there for.

The *Life* magazine article was not quite as harsh on the jury as Rose remembers, but was certainly negative in tone: "The jury filed in. Twelve men and women who had made up their minds and hearts in two hours and nineteen minutes. They did not look at the defendant" (Bedford 1964, 74).

JMD: There was some criticism of the speed of the verdict—two-and-a-half hours, basically. I've had other jurors say, hey, we were there for two weeks and had a long time to think about it.

WR: What are you going to do, go through it [the testimony] all over again? You sit and you listen. . . . You hear it and you make up your mind as you go along. Two and two always ends up four. . . . We were concerned about it being done so quickly, because we talked about it [during the deliberations]. I mentioned that we may be under some criticism for reaching a quick decision, if that's what we're going to do. But I can't see how anybody could not have made up their mind by this time. If you haven't listened to it, what have you been doing? What are you here for? It didn't make any sense at all to me to be ashamed of having spent two hours. You know, we could have spent an hour. But what would have been accomplished if we had spent two or

three days? Another two or three days of people [on the outside] looking at it [and saying], "Wonder why it's taking them so long?"

JMD: Do you feel it was that clear-cut in most of the jurors' minds?

WR: I don't know, I'd like to think so. I wouldn't want to think that
any one of us convinced somebody to change their minds during the
deliberations. I know we had holdouts about the extent of the penalty,
but there was never any doubt as to whether or not he was guilty.
There was never any doubt as to whether he was sane, at the time [of
the murder]. . . . There was one or two who wanted not to give the
death penalty, but some way the decision was reached and they were
convinced that their thinking was wrong.

JMD: What do you think happened [that led Ruby to kill Oswald]?
What do you think was his motivation?

WR: I don't know what goes through a man's mind to cause him to
do such an irrational deed. Why would a person hold up a bank? Maybe
he [the bank robber] needed the money. Maybe he [Ruby] needed the
notoriety. Maybe he needed the fame. Maybe he wanted his name in
the paper.

JMD: What did you think about all of the publicity that the jury got
during the trial? Did you all get some of these nasty letters and phone
calls?

WR: Yeah, I have several letters. Of course, I didn't get the nasty phone
calls that I might have because we didn't answer the telephone a lot. I
got some letters, but most of them were complimentary. I didn't get
any threatening letters. But the publicity—the people were eager to
hear what was going on, and the newspaper, being in the newspaper
business, they wanted to sell newspapers, so they gave it the coverage.

JMD: It was incredible to see all those stories with [the jurors'] ad-
dresses listed.

WR: That frankly surprised me, but I guess we weren't in such a violent world in those days. We didn't have the drive-by shootings and all
the other things that go on.

JMD: Two years later when the Court of Appeals ordered a new trial
for Ruby, do you have memories of what you thought about that?

WR: Well, I was disappointed that they did it, but I took it as I do with
the everyday criminal element who are granted new trials, new hear-

ings, appeals, and all that. The system seems to wear everybody down after awhile, so I was not at all surprised that they would do it, because everybody's entitled to the whole process. But I didn't believe it [a new trial for Ruby] would ever get anywhere. If he got another trial, I figure they would have arrived at the same decision.

Sometimes there's not a lot of use in it [granting a new trial], but if there are serious errors, they need to be corrected.

JMD: Well, of course, the court's reason [for ordering a new trial] was it felt that the trial should have been moved out of Dallas. What do you think about that?

WR: No, I don't think that had any effect on it [the outcome of the trial] at all. That wouldn't have changed any of the evidence, you'd only have new faces looking at it. And if the evidence is still there, and is still valid, they've got to reach the same conclusion. Like I said, two and two is always four.

JMD: It would have been difficult to find a jury of people who didn't see the shooting on television. It was a unique situation.

WR: They couldn't have found that. You know, if you're going to be judged by a jury of your peers, I'd hate to be judged by a panel of people who never knew anything about that [the murder of Oswald]. You'd have to be somewhere under the sea.

JMD: There are still people who like to bring up the conspiracy theories that Ruby was trying to silence Oswald, that they knew each other. Do you give any credence to any of those stories?

WR: No, of course, that was never covered in the trial. It's interesting conjecture and makes a good story, but I never thought there was anything to it.

JMD: Have you ever had any second thoughts about any of this, any kind of rethinking of what happened?

WR: No, the only rethinking I've done is I wish it had happened a couple of years later because then we'd have been in those new "penthouse" quarters that they built in the new courthouse, and [it would have] got us out of that stinky place we were in [laughs]. . . . I haven't given this all that much thought. Down through the years, since all that happened I've never been contacted by anybody who wanted to talk about it in depth. I've run into several aficionados of this whole process who were interested in talking about it. We happened to stay in a bed-and-breakfast back twenty years ago in North Carolina, and it happened that a couple came in, and over dinner it came out that I had been on the Jack Ruby jury. This man was really into all that. He was enthralled. He had the most entertaining evening he'd ever spent, he said, in talking about this [chuckles]. But beyond him and his enthusiasm, I haven't found a lot of people who are really very much interested.

Douglas J. Sowell

D ouglas J. Sowell was the fifth juror selected, and at the time of the trial, he was a mechanic with Braniff Airlines in Dallas. At this writing, he is retired and lives outside of the small East Texas town of Beckville.

JMD: I'll sort of open this by leaving it open-ended. Just tell me what your memories of the trial are and the things that stand out to you as you think back about it now.

DS: Well, it was a lot of people involved to start with. I remember 200 or 300 people waiting to be culled [chuckles], so there were a lot of people there.

A pool of 900 prospective jurors was called to court. Judge Joe Brown shuffled cards bearing the names of the 900, and used the 150 cards that came out on top to draw the names of potential jurors for the trial. The remainder of the prospective jurors were used in other cases (Belli 1964).

And I had never served on a jury, I don't believe, prior to that. I've been on a couple of juries since. But, I remember the waiting and worrying about family. Back in those days, people weren't prepared to not have any income coming in for a great period of time.

And companies, even large companies, didn't pay salaries while you were on jury duty. So that was a worry for me. And I remember when I did get off the case, I found out that everybody in the company had chipped a little money in, I think maybe had gotten some to my wife, I don't know. But it was a lot longer wait than I thought it would be. I didn't think we'd be down there this long.

But, it was . . . it was hard to figure out just what they were gonna keep us around there and do with us, because most of us were convinced that they would never have a trial [in Dallas] because we saw it on TV. . . . I thought it would be moved, and being one of the 400 or 500 people that were brought in for this, I didn't think I'd be picked. I wasn't gonna go there and say anything that they didn't ask me. I was just gonna answer questions on the stand and that's all I did. I think they might have tried to lead me into what I thought about this or that, but I'd just say I didn't have any opinion.

You know, we didn't sit there and judge whether or not he committed the crime, that wasn't what we were there for. We saw that on TV. So it came down to this disease that only a couple of people in the world had ever heard of I think, psychomotor epilepsy, I believe that was it. So I just didn't see where they put on any evidence, or said anything, or convinced anybody that they had a case. And we didn't talk about it when we were in the jury quarters, but we were all wondering the same thing: What are we gonna do here? I mean, we're spending all this time down here, and right off the bat, they brought up this epilepsy thing. Most of us had been around epileptics, we knew something about it, so that was on our minds.

But, there wasn't anything else outstanding, except Belli—he just antagonized everybody. I mean he was just real blunt on his letting us know that we were just country bumpkins down here in Dallas.

JMD: Do you remember some specific comments?

DS: One of the specific things he said close to the end, that we should find this man not guilty based on the fact that it would help our community . . . in the status with the rest of the world, the rest of the U.S., that we should do that just to make Dallas look like a real city rather than a hick town. . . . He hit us pretty hard. He didn't make any friends.

JMD: Do you think that had a negative influence?

DS: Oh, I think it had a negative influence. We did have a couple of persons in the first place that didn't want the death [penalty]. . . . Well, the first round of votes, I think it was two that wouldn't vote for the death penalty. [In his memoir, Max Causey writes three jurors initially voted for a penalty other than death.] Everybody, right off the bat, within five minutes when we got in the jury room, I think we took a vote and we voted guilty. But then when it came to the sentence, we had a couple that didn't want to go the death penalty route. But after a little lecture from Max, we had another vote, and we discussed it a little bit. They just couldn't do it, it was hard for them to do it. But we reminded them that they already told all the judges and everybody else in the whole country that they could give the death penalty. They wouldn't have been on the jury if they'd have said this to start with. So that's why we had such a fast decision.

JMD: Do you recall how long it was?

DS: About fifteen minutes, the best I can remember. Not long. We stayed in there a long time before we told them we did it [chuckles] . . . . We got a lot of criticism for being so quick with the verdict. [It] was about the only thing we could do considering what he had done. So we were pretty strong on doing what was right. We wanted to hear everybody's opinion, but there wasn't anyone standing up for him, that I remember. I don't know of anybody who likes to see somebody put to death, but that's the law, and that's the punishment. And . . . I remember, they made a big deal of that, the lawyers did later I think, about us, that we had fixed minds or something— we were brainwashed, and it was terrible that we came to that conclusion so quick. Well, it wasn't quick. We'd been up there a month and a half [chuckles].

JMD: When you were selected as a juror, you went in with apparently hundreds of other people. But when you were selected, what were your feelings?

DS: Well, I was a little disappointed because I didn't think I'd be selected, but I was gonna be willing to go ahead and do my duty if they did select me. . . . We'd been down there long enough that I was tired of it. . . . The jury selection took about two weeks, seemed to me like, maybe not quite that long. But they'd just pick one each day, take all day, and maybe pick one juror. And I think one day there, they picked two, and we thought that was great. But, see, we were locked in once we were selected for the jury, we couldn't go home or anything.

JMD: So the selection process took almost as long as the trial itself?

DS: Oh, yeah. [The jury selection process took fourteen days, as 163 prospective jurors were questioned. The trial altogether ran twenty-six days, from February 17 to March 14, 1964.]

JMD: Did you know when you got the summons that it was likely to be for the Ruby trial?

DS: We knew that. When they sent the summons out, I think the media and everybody let us know that they were gonna bring in about 500 people, so they'd have plenty of people to talk to. I don't know whether they brought that many in the first round or not. I did shuttle back and forth until they actually picked me.

JMD: What do you remember about being sequestered?

DS: Well, it wasn't too bad. We had a couple of good bailiffs, a woman and a man. They were strong-minded, strong people and didn't put up with any foolishness from the press or anybody else. . . . He [bailiff Bo Mabra] made it easy for us. He monitored the TV, and chopped the papers up to where we could read what we could. He had to do all that. And when we went out to eat, we had to slip out, and they'd block the road some place, block the press out. We got to go to North Dallas and eat most of the time at the nicer restaurants.

JMD: And you were actually quartered in the courthouse, is that right?

DS: Above the jail, I believe, the seventh floor.

JMD: Tell me how you were selected as juror.

DS: Well, I was called in there, and . . . [assistant defense attorney Joe] Tonahill was doing the questioning. He asked me my name and where I worked and all this bit, and he said, "And what part of the country are you from. You sound like a country boy," or something like that. And I told him I grew up in San Augustine; it's just a little community south of here. And he was in practice at that time in Jasper I believe, and he hit [the table] just like that, and said, "I like this ol' boy. I believe he could make me a good juror," something to that extent. "I'll take him." And he looked around at Belli, and they all made a decision right there. But he tried to make a nice statement, and make me feel good. He went ahead and said, "We're just next-door neighbors. I grew up down there, too. . . ."

I guess I was picked quicker than any juror, because some of them were on the stand all day and some even the second day. But I was just there a few minutes, and that was strictly because Tonahill thought he'd make an impression on me. You know, talking about "this ol' East Texas boy," like I was his long-lost son or something.

In an excerpt from the *voir dire* questioning of Sowell, Tonahill spoke to Sowell as if he were a friend of a friend:

Tonahill: Do you have a sister named Pauline?

Sowell: No.

Tonahill: What are your sisters' names?

Sowell: Mamie Joyce and Jackie Wayne.

Tonahill: Do you know Pauline?

Sowell: I don't know her, no.

Tonahill: Is there another Sowell family around here?

Sowell: There are many . . . as I understand it.

Tonahill: Some in Jasper?

Sowell: Some in Jasper.

Tonahill: Do you know Joe Fisher?

Sowell: No, I don't know Joe Fisher. I left San Augustine when I was sixteen.

Tonahill: Mr. Sowell, we East Texas and California lawyers and Jack Ruby will accept you on the jury because we feel you will make a good juror (Statement of Facts, 1383, 1388, 1389).

JMD: Was there any other reason you think you were picked, other than that?

DS: I don't think I'd have been picked if Tonahill hadn't been the one doing it, because I don't know whether I could have held back my feelings [toward] Belli if he'd started talking to me. It would have probably boiled over because he was terrible to even be around, that guy was. I don't think much of Belli.

Belli (1964, p. 133) wrote: "Sowell also indicated what we regarded as a healthy skepticism about press coverage of news events, particularly healthy because of the prejudiced way this event was being covered in Dallas. 'Sometimes they write 'em before they think,' he said with a grin. 'I don't go much on press reports.'"

JMD: Was it just the comments he [Belli] made about Dallas?
DS: Those things, just like we were a bunch of dummies, you know. And, I don't know, everything he said was something bad about us, we there in Dallas, you know.
JMD: And this was during the trial?
DS: Yeah, even when he was selecting jurors, apparently he would get smart with 'em and everything.

Authors John Kaplan and John R. Waltz noted (1965, p. 71): "In a New York interview, he (Belli) introduced a theme that was to recur again and again. He informed reporters that 'The people of Dallas, perhaps unconsciously, have to have a sacrifice in order to cleanse themselves. They feel that the best way to prove that it [Dallas] is a law-abiding community would be give him a fair trial—and then hang him.' Ruby's attorneys seemed to be following the old saw that the best defense is a good attack—but with a difference. The counterattack was not to be against the loathed [Lee Harvey] Oswald; it was to be against the entire citizenry of Dallas."

JMD: Was it also a matter of Belli's demeanor?
DS: Yeah, he was too flashy. We didn't need that. I mean, he was like a popcorn salesman at the fair or something, you know [chuckles]. He didn't give me the impression he was a lawyer. He didn't conduct himself like a lawyer, even during the trial. It's terrible. But that's just things, that's the way I see 'em . . . He was just too flashy. Belli hurt his case . . . he was right, those people in Dallas, they weren't his kind of people.

"Probably the most powerful reason for prejudice against Ruby, on the issues that really counted, was the behavior of his counsel and the statements attacking Dallas which Melvin Belli made in and out of court. Belli himself appeared to recognize this during the change-of-venue hearing when he cited as prejudicial publicity the newspaper reports of his statements of the day before. The chances were that many Dallas residents who entertained no particular ill will toward Ruby might be so stung by Belli's assaults on their city that, if selected as jurors, they would take out their animosity toward Belli, consciously or not, in the only way they could—on his client" (Kaplan and Waltz 1965, 81).

JMD: To read the press accounts of this, it seems like it was kind of a circus. But I don't know if you all were aware of that.

DS: All we had was what we saw while we were in there being quizzed, being selected. That's all we were privy to, we didn't know what went on the rest of the time. And the jurors that were selected and brought in after—I was number five, and we had another eight, ten or twelve days of selection going on—so when these jurors came in, we didn't talk about what happened with them or anything. We were very careful not to talk about the case. We were friendly, we would play dominoes, and do all those things, but we didn't read anything, hear anything or talk about anything that happened.

Contemporary press accounts were full of colorful courtroom antics. At one point, Belli was examining Texas Highway Patrol Captain M. C. Blount and the exchange became heated. "Are you trying to shout me down?" Belli demanded. Blount replied, in a booming voice, "I'm a pretty good shouter!" Belli shot back, "You're a pretty good shooter, too, are you?" ("Shouter, Shooter," 1964)

During a pretrial hearing, Belli accused assistant district attorney Bill Alexander of referring to Ruby as a "Jew boy," although most people in the courtroom thought Alexander said "Jewish boy" (Kaplan and Waltz 1965, 59).

Later, in a tense moment during jury selection, Belli exclaimed, "Alexander can last only four hours without using such words as 'peasant' and 'Jew boy' and now he's using the Lord's name in vain!" It was not clear from the story if or how Alexander had blasphemed ("7th Juror," 1964).

JMD: And out of your own sense of obligation or sense of duty that you knew you were not to do that [speak about the case]?

DS: That's right. We knew that, and everybody does. They'll tell you that you're not to be talking about the case. Any juror does that.

JMD: Did the bailiff or anyone stay around to make sure you didn't?

DS: The bailiffs are always in our presence, somewhere close by. But we didn't have anyone try to talk about it. We all knew what we saw [during the trial].

JMD: Of course, there was a lot of feeling before the trial happened that it would not be held in Dallas, that it would be moved to another city. Thinking back about it now, do you think that might have been a better way to go, to change the venue?

DS: Well, I didn't see anything in any of the jurors that would indicate that they might be partial or felt any pressure to make a decision because we were in Dallas. I don't think you would have had any better jury than the one we were on. I don't think anyone wanted to convict a man for murder, unless he did it. We had a pretty strong group there. When we, after discussing it awhile, took a vote of hands, we had a couple of people who wouldn't vote the death penalty. So we had to discuss it some, and they came around pretty quickly.

JMD: Belli, of course, had hoped that the trial would be moved out of Dallas, and one of his major criticisms was that the members of the jury were too much alike, that there were no Jews, no union members . . . .

DS: I was a member of a union.

JMD: What union were you a member of?

DS: Machinists union, Braniff Airways, all the mechanics were in the machinists union.

Belli (1964, p. 118) commented on the Dallas County jury selection process: "What it produced was a panel that was a reflection of the Dallas Establishment, the white Anglo-Saxon Protestants whose values the oligarchy held, who identified themselves with the white Anglo-Saxon Protestant oligarchy. 'There's not a union man on this list,' I moaned to Joe (Tonahill)."

JMD: Looking back, do you feel it would have been better . . . Ruby, of course, was Jewish . . .

DS: You know, I didn't know that. Up until that time in my life, I had not very much knowledge of what a Jew was, and didn't realize they were a minority group, or anything like that, or some of the things they've had to go through over the years. I was thirty-three years old, but I didn't know.

JMD: So, at the time, you didn't realize [that Ruby was Jewish]?

DS: I didn't realize it, and it wasn't brought out at any time. I don't remember them bringing it out before the jury, the lawyers I mean. [However, as previously noted, Belli did complain during the trial about the prosecuting attorneys referring to Ruby as a "Jew boy," a charge the prosecution denied.]

JMD: So you don't think it was a factor in the outcome of the trial, that you had twelve people, all white, Protestant people, middle-class?

DS: Well, in years past . . . I realize that race has to do with every trial. If you have an all-white, or all-black, or all-Jew [jury], whatever, there's going to be people looking and seeing that they have the right representation for each group. Before that, there wasn't anything in the newspaper to get you thinking, or even consider the fact that we were all white. It didn't mean anything to us really. We were just citizens of that county and that's why we wound up on the jury.

JMD: I'm going to ask you your other impressions of some of the people in the trial. Did you get any impression at all of Jack Ruby from having participated in the trial?

DS: Oh, yeah. Everything that was brought up was revealing. Just when they were talking about him, what a fine fellow he was, good businessman, he would carry sandwiches down to the policemen, give 'em tickets to his club. Well, I figured out pretty fast what his clubs were, and he brought that poor little girl in there one day that was pregnant, I think [Karen Bennett Carlin, "Little Lynn," one of Ruby's dancers]. Back in those days, that was before it became cool to do that [become pregnant outside of marriage].

JMD: How about Judge Brown, who had sort of a reputation as a flamboyant fellow?

DS: Well, I don't remember anything. He didn't impress me one way or the other, other than just being the judge. He'd have to pull the lawyers over to talk to them every once in awhile. I think he handled it very well. There didn't seem to be any problems, he didn't let it get out of hand. He made 'em stay with the subject.

Judge Brown had been elected to the position of criminal district court judge in 1956, and had twice been re-elected. He had the reputation of running a "loose courtroom," in which he relied more on a friendly relationship with the attorneys than upon formality to maintain order. He was considered fair, if not overly learned. Thirty-four of his cases had been reviewed by the Texas Court of Criminal Appeals, with ten reversals due to judicial errors, a relatively high ratio, and significant because the appeals court eventually ordered a retrial of the Ruby case in 1966. Ironically, in view of Belli's complaints, Brown was generally considered a defense judge and ruled against the prosecution in the majority of decisions (Kaplan and Waltz 1965).

JMD: Belli commented in his book that Judge Brown ruled too often in favor of the prosecution in the trial. Do you have any recollections along those lines?

DS: No, I think he ran a pretty good show, pretty good trial. He didn't speak up on anything that would jar me or get me thinking in a different direction or anything. Belli was his own worst enemy, I believe, because he'd get off on these tangents trying to make us believe that we were going to make Dallas a town known for unfair justice, or something like that. He was trying to make us feel like if we didn't find him innocent, then we were going to be a black eye on the whole city of Dallas. So he didn't have a personality that was very likable as much as you can learn about the personality of someone if you sit there and listen to them. I tried not to let that influence me in my voting. In fact, the vote was so much one-sided, you really couldn't feel like you were out of line.

JMD: Henry Wade? Do you have any memories of him?

DS: I knew a lot about Henry Wade before I went in there and he was just what I expected. He was just a rough old lawyer, tough, rough, and pretty proud of himself. And he had reason to be proud. But he wasn't easy to get around. He could chew Belli up in a minute. Belli didn't think so, but he could, you know.

JMD: Do you think, perhaps, because he was from Dallas, he was a Texan, that he had a better rapport with the jurors?

DS: Probably, probably. We knew him and he knew how to get the attention of the jurors. I think he was the lawyer for it, he did the job.

JMD: You mentioned, during the deliberations, the role that Max played. Do you have memories of him as the foreman of the jury?

DS: Oh, yes. That was the first thing we did, elect a foreman.

JMD: How did that come about?

DS: Well, Max was the first juror picked. He'd been there longer than the rest of us. He had seniority [chuckles]. He'd been locked up by himself for a couple of days, I think. And he was just . . . he had a personality that was easy to appreciate. He made sure we didn't get onto the subject [of the trial] and stayed away from the case. We elected him foreman right off. . . . Most of us had been around him for awhile . . . So, we had an election, and I think it was unanimous. I don't remember, but I believe it was. And he knew he was the foreman and he had responsibilities, and [before Causey was elected foreman] he saw that we stayed in line. We played certain games, and certain games we couldn't. We didn't do any gambling, all those things. He made those rules, I guess [chuckles].

JMD: No gambling. That's interesting.

DS: No gambling. No, we played "42," and dominoes, and cards. Watched a little TV. The days are long when you have a twenty-four-hour day and you spend maybe four hours in court.

JMD: Did he [Causey] more or less act as the leader of the jury before he was elected foreman, as the trial was going on?

DS: Yes, his personality was such that he would assume a leadership role if it was open or it needed to be filled. He was just that type person. In my recollection, he was a supervisor-type on the job. As far as him having a group stay around him, or spend time with him, playing off together, there wasn't any of that going on at all. We had so little time to get to know one another. Anything we might be talking about might be our family, or something like that. There wasn't any real need for someone to step up and be a leader.

JMD: You touched on this, the insanity defense, the disease that the defense portrayed as being the reason for what happened. Obviously, this just didn't make much of an impression.

DS: No, no. Belli explained to us what psychomotor epilepsy is. You know what that is: You're under an epileptic seizure, and you will go ahead and do something, and maybe not plan it. But you will do something while you're under the seizure not knowing what you've done. Well, I don't think anyone bought that. In fact, we had very little discussion on it. It was ridiculous. You know, if he's under epileptic [seizure] . . . Everybody has been around epileptics. I grew up with one, my first cousin, he'd have seizures. But epileptics don't go out and get a gun and go kill somebody while they're under seizure. In the first place, they [the seizures] don't last that long, most of the seizures don't. Too many things . . . it just didn't impress us at all.

JMD: What were your thoughts on the psychiatrists who testified on Ruby's behalf?

DS: I found that they weren't very good witnesses. They seemed to me to believe that we, the jurors, were believing all the things that they were telling us. You know, just like we weren't bright enough to figure all this stuff out—just listen to them and just vote their way, it seemed to me. They didn't have very much confidence in us having very much education, I guess. They seemed to try to put us on the defensive that, if we're smart, if we're educated, we'd recognize this great piece of help in the medical world, this EEG. Well, most of us understand what an EEG does. I got the impression that the psychiatrists felt we were incapable of understanding the EEG.

But, anyway, they didn't seem to want to bring any . . . I wondered really why they didn't bring in some people [who also were diagnosed as suffering from psychomotor epilepsy] other than just this one [Ruby]. . . . I mean, here we have a good, new piece of equipment, [an] aid to the medical profession and they didn't give us anyone that they had found in this situation before. They didn't bring anybody in that has been tested for this except Ruby. You know, they didn't help us a lot. They had a sophisticated piece of equipment they could prove anything with, if they're staying on the straight and narrow and believing in what they're doing.

JMD: So if they had brought someone else forward who was in a similar situation . . .

DS: Oh, yeah. If they'd have brought someone else in that had this problem and went into seizures and continued on and walked a half a mile or whatever, or twenty or thirty feet. [Ruby walked 339½ feet from the downtown Western Union office to the entry of the police station ramp where he shot Oswald.] I'm sure there are some epileptics that have a mild case probably where they could continue to walk, but I don't know of any.

JMD: Do you remember much about Dr. Gibbs, who was the last psychiatrist, in fact, the last person to testify in the trial? They had built him up a lot during the trial, and then he made a dramatic appearance . . .

DS: Yeah, he didn't come up with anything. He didn't give us anything new, did he? He came in with this EEG and they had built this thing up and what it does and all this, and then he didn't bring any proof with him. Ruby's the only one, as far as we know, that had this condition and they were able to pick it up with this EEG. He [Mr. Belli] didn't bring fifteen or twenty people in there, other psychiatrists, or other medical people, or even other patients. He just didn't bring 'em in any numbers at all to help prove his case.

JMD: He [Ruby] was apparently pretty quick to get in a fight, a pretty aggressive fellow. Was there any testimony about that quality of his personality?

DS: No, no there wasn't. It came out someway that he beat up on young women, and girls, and had complete control of his strippers and all that, but as far as fighting with somebody his size, I don't remember them bringing that out.

JMD: If you'd been conducting the defense for Ruby, how might you have done it differently? What would have been more persuasive?

DS: I would have stuck with the fact that Ruby felt that he was doing the country a favor—patriotism. I think that he felt that everybody would thank him for killing ol' Oswald because he [Ruby] was a patriot to the country. I think I would have not even had psychiatrists around. I think they should have tried to prove it through the fact that Ruby was being very patriotic in going out there and killing the man that killed the president. And he had a lot of following in that area. A lot of people believed that, and thought that's the way it ought to have been done. I think he could have built a pretty good case. A lot of people were saying that he [Ruby] did the right thing, and they should have played on that. But they [the defense] didn't bring anything else with this psychomotor epilepsy thing, that's for sure. That fell on its face.

JMD: This comes up constantly, the conspiracy theories, Ruby killed Oswald to silence him, he was hired by the mob, they knew each other, this or that. Do you give any credibility to that at all?

DS: Not at all. I never have and never will. I mean, there's too many factors people like to leave out. The fact that [Dallas police officer J. D.] Tippit was killed; he [Oswald] had an apartment rented over in Oak Cliff, all that stuff. I don't give any credence to any of that. They keep bringing it up, but these people, they don't have anything to go on.

JMD: Well, Ruby had no chance to get away whatsoever. If someone had hired him to do such a job . . . it makes no sense to me that someone would have a motivation to do it [kill Oswald] under those circumstances.

DS: No, the only motivation that he had. . . . What he said, or what they claimed, you know, [was] that he was just in remorse [over the assassination of President Kennedy], and he thought he'd be a hero in the public's eye if he did it. I believe he thought that, I really do. I think that motivated him, that he thought rather than being a murderer, he'd be a hero.

JMD: Did you see the murder of Oswald on television?

DS: I probably had seen it on TV a number of times because they reran that thing quite a few times. I'm sure I saw it.

JMD: But you didn't see it live, as it happened?

DS: As it happened, live, no.

JMD: Did you ever have any threatening calls, letters, anything that came in either during or after the trial?

DS: No, I don't think so . . . and I only had a few reporters there at the house when I got home. We got in the car and left, went for a drive, went to Lake Dallas and drove around.

Bought us a lot up there. . . . But the media didn't make it so hard that the wives or the husbands, whoever was at home, had to fight 'em continually. She [Mrs. Sowell] went about doing her job.

BERNICE SOWELL: Well, as soon as the verdict was announced, you called, or had someone call, seems like you called, and told me to go to Mother's and stay there. And so that's what I did. I don't know who called the house, or who came to the house. You came to Mother's, after you got free.

DS: But they did come to see you, some reporters did, during the trial, didn't they, from time to time and quiz you a little?

BS: Well, it was actually during the selection, I guess, after you had been selected.

JMD: But, you got no . . . there were no threats coming in from nuts?

DS: I don't believe we got anything. Some of 'em did, and I heard about it.

JMD: Mr. [Robert] Flechtner, whom I talked to yesterday, said for some reason they got quite a few.

DS: I don't know why they didn't get me. They probably couldn't have caught me, except the wife was home all the time.

BS: Well, I would have been gone quite a bit, you know. I worked.

DS: And I worked a lot of hours, and a lot of odd hours, at that time. I might go in and work twenty-four hours straight, something like that.

JMD: Did the publicity disturb you at all?

DS: Not really.

JMD: It's amazing to me . . . Boy, the focus on the individual jurors was so terrific in this trial.

DS: Well, I know now, I've [served as a juror on] other cases. I went on a federal case here awhile back in Tyler—it was an income tax evasion case—and that judge kept us around and told us—we convicted the guy—to be careful and to let him know if we get a phone call, threat or anything, he wanted to know about it. They do watch that.

JMD: The Criminal Court of Appeals overturned the [Ruby] decision in 1966, and this was because the trial was not moved out of Dallas. Do you remember your reaction to that?

DS: When was that, '66? I probably didn't even know about it. I was living in Seattle in '66 and '67. I was up there buying airplanes for the company [Braniff].

JMD: In talking to [juror] Glenn Holton, who was a postman then, and is a postman now, I got the impression with him that he almost literally had not thought about this at all since the day the trial was over. It was just not a big deal to him in any way, shape, or form.

DS: It wasn't a big deal with any of us, I don't think. [But] I'm surprised about all the media attention and everything on certain trials nowadays. Our case was bigger.

JMD: Can you imagine what it would be like today?

DS: Oh, you'd have to hold it somewhere out in West Texas. There wouldn't be any room in Dallas to hold all the cars and stuff. But I never thought about it a lot. It was comforting to know that he stayed in jail, you know. He stayed there. He wasn't out doing anything until he died.

JMD: Do you ever give the trial much thought? Is it something you think about very often? Or maybe just when someone brings it up?

DS: Well, I don't think about it a lot, no. Back when he [Mr. Ruby] was still living, I knew he was under the death sentence, and I was one of the jurors, and it was a relief when he died, I have to say. You know, because . . . it bothered me, it bothers me, to give someone the death sentence on something. But I can do it, and when I read of the horrific things that some people are doing to their little kids, I think I could be strong on one of those juries. But, no, it just kind of faded away over the years, I guess.

JMD: Is it a burden to . . .

DS: It's a burden to be on a jury and have to hand down the death penalty. You know, you always have a small bit of question in your mind, whether or not you're playing God, or whatever. You don't forget it, down through the years.

JMD: Has anything over the years caused you to have second thoughts about anything or look at it differently in any way?

DS: No, I've never had a problem either way. Most people that I've been around all these years don't know that I served on that jury. I tell some people, you know, close friends or somebody. But they're amazed to find now that they're talking to a Ruby juror. You've got to find people who are sixty years old. If you're talking to a thirty-year-old, they say, "What's that?"

JMD: What do they ask you about when it comes up?

DS: I don't know. Nothing particular. They're amazed they know somebody who was in a big trial like that, you know, and can't hardly believe that I'm putting it on 'em straight.

Robert J. "Bob" Flechtner

Robert J. "Bob" Flechtner was the sixth juror selected, and at the time of the trial, he was a salesman for Clampitt Paper in Dallas. At the time of this writing, he is an executive with Padgett Printing, also in Dallas.

JMD: What are your memories of the trial? In general, what things stand out to you?

RF: I believe I was the seventh one picked [actually sixth] and when I went in to where the other six [five] were, they were so happy because another juror had been picked, because they'd been there several days. I remember we were pretty well guarded for fear of somebody trying to get us, I don't know why. At the time, they didn't have jury quarters, per se. We just stayed on the seventh floor of the jail, and we actually stayed in cells. Whereas now, I think they've got a building downtown and on the top of it, they've got a place for jurors to stay. I've never been up there, but I'm sure they're better than [what we had]. But I remember we drank jailhouse coffee, and, of course, you couldn't watch TV [news programs], and you couldn't read anything in the paper. They'd give you the newspaper and it'd be all cut up. And there wasn't much to read, there wasn't much to do. And the time went by very slowly, I do remember that.

A *Dallas Morning News* article at the time of the trial described the jurors' quarters in Dallas County's Criminal Courts Building this way: "Max Causey, first juror picked in the Jack Ruby trial, will be housed in an 8-foot square bedroom furnished with a bed, lavatory and commode. His room, like all the others to be used by jurors in the Ruby case, opens off a hall which has a lounge at the far end" ("Lone Ruby Juror," 1964).

An article by Jim Lehrer, the public television commentator, then a reporter for the *Dallas Times Herald*, noted: "If Mr. Causey wants to see the outside world from his locked room, he may go over to the east wall to the windows. The view, however, is not the choicest. He will see only the two-yard breezeway between the Criminal Courts Building and the Records Building next door. Its main inhabitants are pigeons" (Lehrer, "Juror Faces," 1964. The full article appears on pp. 127–29).

JMD: Did you stay in the "cells" the entire time?

RF: Yeah. I was locked up seventeen days and nights, and we stayed on the seventh floor. And it wasn't like you were locked up in a cell, understand. It was just that's the only place they had to keep us. . . . You know, the doors were open and all that, and there was a place that we could all sit. And we all kind of got "cabin fever," and we wanted to go out to eat, so we got 'em to take us out to eat. And I know one night somebody threatened us or something, and it scared 'em and they didn't want to take us out anymore. But they'd take us to cafeterias and they'd call ahead and have us, you know, be off in a room somewhere, and I remember my wife bringing my kids down and, of course, they couldn't come over, they could just see me. And I remember the two bailiffs, Bo Mabra and Nell [Tyler]. They were both just wonderful people, very accommodating, you know, they tried to keep us comfortable, and they were just super people.

JMD: When you were selected for the jury, were you unhappy about that, or what was your reaction?

RF: No, it was funny. Like I told you, the first day I went down there, it was the day I reported for work for Clampitt Paper, and they were joking about it, and they said, "They won't pick you." And, of course, we were in this hall, and there were quite a few people, and you just moved down the seats as they would call you in. Yeah, I was kind of shocked I was picked, but I mean, it didn't scare me or worry me or anything.

JMD: You probably didn't realize how long it [the trial] would take at that time, either.

RF: No, you didn't have any idea. I didn't know what was going to happen.

JMD: When you were called for jury duty, did you suspect it might be for that trial?

RF: No, not really, I just went down [to the courthouse]. And I've served many, many times since then. Many times. Yeah, I've been called so many times, you can't believe it.

JMD: You know, it seems like the same people are called over and over again. I've been called once in my life.

RF: Well, when Judge Brown was alive, they kept calling me year after year, and I went down there to see him, and said, "I've served a lifetime of jury duty down here," and he excused me two or three times. But I was there year before last.

JMD: Why do you think you were selected [for the Ruby trial jury]?

RF: I don't know, maybe they thought I was very truthful and straightforward. I don't know, I really don't know why.

Belli wrote this note about Flechtner in his trial book: "Shriner. Diamond in tie. Hair slicked back. 29. Salesman. Got couple of nice smiles [from Flechtner]. I like him; therefore, he liked us. . . . He looked like a nice, neat *liberal* [Belli's emphasis] guy. I'm surprised, though, he was for capital punishment. He didn't move hands so *must* [Belli's emphasis] have been sincere" (Belli 1964, 136).

Belli believed he could watch a potential juror's hands to determine how he would vote on giving the death penalty. He said that if a juror kept his hands steady when he said he could vote death, he would do it. He believed if a juror twisted his hands as he said he could vote for capital punishment, he wouldn't actually do so (Kaplan and Waltz 1965).

JMD: You were a Shriner at that time?

RF: I was a Mason, yeah.

JMD: Is it Mason or Shriner?

RF: Well, see you've got to be a Mason, then you've got to go Scottish Rite or York Rite before you can become a Shriner.

JMD: And you still maintain that membership?

RF: Yeah.

JMD: One of his [Belli's] notes on you was "nice liberal guy." Was "liberal" a description of your political feelings at that time, or is that something he projected on to you?

RF: Well, I don't know what he meant by "liberal." I remember they asked me if I could give him the death penalty if they proved it, you know. And I asked if it's the law, and he said yes, and I said, well, I've got to uphold the law, so I could do it. So I guess that's where he got me being "liberal."

JMD: Well, he spent several paragraphs commenting on you.

RF: Well, I guess probably because we were brothers in the Masonry, but maybe not.

JMD: I didn't know he was a Mason as well.

RF: Oh, sure.

JMD: The trial itself, in reading about it . . . it seems as if it was kind of a circus atmosphere.

RF: There were so many things that happened while we were there that we didn't know happened till afterwards. Like there was a jailbreak and they were chasing somebody around. There were several things like that that happened. Like I say, they didn't let us read the newspapers, or see TV, or anything. . . . I'm a car nut, and I remember one time I told Bo, I said, "I tell you what, you get me some automobile magazines to read or something, or I'm walking out of here." And, man, I got a bunch of magazines.

The jailbreak occurred as seven prisoners got loose in the courthouse, brushing past one of Ruby's strippers who had been called to testify and causing her to faint. But a lot of the Ruby trial's reputation for zaniness may be attributed to the comments of assistant defense attorney Joe Tonahill, the bearlike East Texan. In posing a question, Tonahill would begin, "When that Communist Oswald was shot . . ." When District Attorney Henry Wade objected, Tonahill continued, "When that lily-of-the-valley Oswald was shot . . ." Once, Tonahill inquired of a prospective juror, "Would you feel un-Texan if you were on the first jury to send a man to the electric chair for killing a Communist?" Belli later admitted, "I guess I let Joe go too far with that cornball stuff" (Kaplan and Waltz 1965, 102–103).

Belli himself more subtly raised Oswald's Communist leanings when he asked Dallas police officer James Leavelle if he had seen a photograph of Oswald giving a "Communist salute." Leavelle said he had seen the photo, and then, under questioning by assistant district attorney Bill Alexander, admitted he wouldn't recognize a Communist salute if he saw one (Statement of Facts, 195, 204).

The opposing attorneys constantly sniped at one another. Belli and Tonahill would pronounce assistant district attorney A. D. [Jim] Bowie's name as "boy," and Wade and his men would refer to Belli (pronounced "bell-eye") as "Mr. Belly." (Kaplan and Waltz 1965, 102–103)

JMD: I'm going to ask you your impressions of some of the people involved in the trial, and, of course, first of all, Jack Ruby. In observing him during the trial and in the testimony that was given, what impressions did you form of him?

RF: I don't know, as I remember, Jack was real quiet. I don't know that I ever made a judgment of him. . . . I remember Belli, because he was very flamboyant. I don't know, I think he was trying to make Jack a hero.

JMD: Belli was very critical of the city of Dallas, called Dallas the "city of shame." [This was in the immediate aftermath of the trial.]

RF: He wrote a book that I read, and I think I was the only one he had anything nice to say about. And he was very critical of Dallas, said we were a bunch of hatemongers, I don't know what all, it's been a long time since I read it.

Belli wrote: "I did like Flechtner and, except for my brief outburst of anger at all twelve jurors when, after a shockingly brief time, they had voted death for Jack Ruby. I think he is the type of person I could always get along with. His smile was boyishly friendly, his manner modest. And it is as true of juror selection as it is of personal contact—the people you like tend to like you. In any other city in any other case I think Flechtner could have been a warmly sympathetic juror" (Belli 1964, 136).

JMD: But you don't recall him making comments like that during the trial?
RF: No, I don't remember him saying anything about Dallas during the trial, it's been so long ago.

Most of Belli's anti-Dallas comments came during pretrial hearings, early in the jury selection process, and after the trial. In fact, early in the presentation of testimony, a *Dallas Times Herald* article noted: "Predictions that the courtroom battling would calm down have proved—thus far—to be accurate. The atmosphere is so cordial that spectators and newsmen new to the proceedings are believing prior stories of heated courtroom antics were a hoax. . . . Objections are few and far between and spoken in normal tones rather than shouts" ("Cordiality Prevails" 1964).

JMD: He [Belli] thought even as jury selection began that the trial would be moved to another location outside of Dallas. As you look back on it, do you think it would have been better had the trial been moved out of Dallas, or do you think it was the proper thing to have it in Dallas?
RF: I don't know if would have made a whole lot of difference. I mean, it was pretty well national news what happened, so I don't know how you could move it anywhere else. I don't know, it's hard to say whether it would have made any difference. You know, Belli was pretty arrogant.

Although it became apparent as jury selection progressed that the trial would be held in Dallas, Judge Brown did not officially rule against the defense's motion for a change of venue until the court convened on March 4, 1964, the day when the presentation of evidence in the case began. The judge's first action that day was to rule against the change of venue (Statement of Facts, 1).

JMD: Belli felt that jury represented the establishment of Dallas, what he called the "oligarchy," all Protestant, middle-class, and lamented the fact there were no Jews on the jury because Ruby was Jewish. Have you ever had any thoughts on that?

RF: I don't even think I knew he was Jewish until after the fact, to be honest with you, because I just never even thought about what he was. If he had two heads, I don't think it would have made a difference. That was one thing I didn't even know about, and then, later on, after the thing was over, I realized it because I got some hate mail from some Jewish people.

JMD: You didn't feel, and as far as you know none of the other jury members felt, any pressure from the powerful people of Dallas, whoever they may have been at that time, to come down with one sort of verdict or another?

RF: No, no. You know, I was pretty young [twenty-nine years old] . . . I was just trying to make a living for my family, and that was all I was worried about. As far as any Dallas politics, I certainly wasn't involved in that in any shape or fashion.

JMD: Yeah, I've seen your picture in some of the newspapers at the time. You looked like you were in high school.

RF: [chuckles] Yeah.

JMD: Do you have memories of [Henry] Wade?

RF: Sure. I'd heard of Henry Wade all my life. He was just, kind of, Dallas.

JMD: He had a good rapport with the people on the jury?

RF: Oh, yeah, I think he did. I think all the lawyers did. You know, they tried to get along with us. My gosh, they were trying to win a case.

Wade, who graduated with highest honors from the University of Texas Law School in 1938, had served as the district attorney for Dallas County since 1951. Wade's prosecutor's office was regarded as the most able and honest in Dallas history. He was known as a career DA without political ambition, unless it was to become a federal judge. In his career, he had asked for the death penalty in twenty-four cases and had been successful twenty-three times (Kaplan and Waltz 1965).

JMD: It was an interesting contrast, though, Belli and Wade in the same courtroom.

RF: Oh, yeah, there was, tremendous. Oh, there wasn't any comparison. I mean, they were as different as daylight and dark. You know, that's funny. [They're] the only two that I remember. I know there were some others [attorneys].

JMD: Do you have any memories of Judge Brown? He was kind of a legendary figure. How did he conduct the trial?

RF: Well, I think he was very strong and he didn't put up with any baloney. He kept good order. I think he did a really good job.

JMD: Do you have memories of Max Causey, who served on the jury, and was the foreman?

RF: Yeah, I'm not sure I'd know Max if I ran into him today [Mr. Causey died in September 1997]. Everybody on the jury was pretty straightforward, they were nice people.

JMD: We talked about how you felt about being sequestered. It was something that was obviously not a pleasant experience for you.

RF: Well, it got to be. I mean, after being locked up a long time away from your family. I'm just wondering if you were locked up today if it would be that bad. But, I mean, to be kept in there, and not have much to read or do . . . I think they were worried that somebody was going to do something to us. That's what I think. Why anybody would try to do anything to us, I don't know.

JMD: It was a crazy time. And, in some respects, it's more so today.

RF: Oh, I think it is more so. I think you would have to worry about it more today than then. Yeah.

JMD: Of course, Belli presented an insanity defense, that Ruby was a man out of control.

RF: Psychomotor epilepsy. Instantaneous . . . what did he say? It was he was crazy for a few seconds or something.

JMD: What did you make of that?

RF: Golly, I don't know. I think we just put it all together, and all pretty much decided that he was guilty.

JMD: It obviously did not make an impression, [as] you were not convinced.

RF: I wish I could remember more of it. I guess you put things like that out of your mind. I don't know.

JMD: He [Ruby] had a history of being a guy who lost his temper and got into fights.

RF: Well, you know, it was surprising to me because I've lived in Dallas all my life, and Jack Ruby owned a club, which they brought out. I had no idea that he owned a club. I knew of the club, because Dallas was very different back then, and it was pretty risqué for Dallas. I think it was called the Colony Club, I can't even remember. [Ruby's club at the time of the shooting was the Carousel Club.] It was down across from the Adolphus [Hotel]. But I remember everybody talked about one of the strippers there. Her name was Chris Colt, "the lady with the 45s." Of course, I don't think anybody in Dallas didn't know about Chris Colt, and then when they said he owned that club where she worked . . .

JMD: You started to put things together.

RF: Yeah. I didn't know it till the trial.

JMD: As you know, there is endless speculation about all of this, the conspiracy theories. People talk about Ruby committing the crime to silence Oswald, that they knew each other somehow, that there was a mob connection with Ruby. Do you give any credibility to any of those conspiracy theories having to do with Ruby?

RF: No. I think Ruby felt sorry for Jack's kids, and for Jacqueline Kennedy, and [Ruby] just got himself all worked up and maybe somebody helped get him worked up, who knows? And I think he just went down there and shot Oswald and thought he was going to be a hero. And he thought he was doing the right thing, and our society says he didn't do the right thing. And I think that's just the plain-and-simple of it. I think he just let his emotions run away with him. If we all did that, this would be a hell of a place to live.

JMD: Do you have any reason to think somebody might have worked him up into a frenzy or is that just something you think is possible?

RF: I guess it could be possible. Maybe they knew that he was that sort of person, perhaps. I don't know who it would have been. Maybe somebody just said, "Jack, you know, somebody ought to go down there and shoot him." And Jack says, "Well, you know, I could do that, because all the policemen know me, I go down there all the time."

And maybe . . . Who knows? But I think really, maybe, he just got to thinking about it.

JMD: Why were the psychiatrists who testified for Ruby not more convincing?

RF: It seems to me that when they were up there, they were saying that he [Ruby] went nuts for thirty seconds and killed a guy. I mean, it was like, he was crazy for maybe an hour or so, and then he was all right. As far as Belli, it seemed to me Belli was trying to make Ruby a hero, rather than [acknowledging Ruby's] taking a person's life, you know. The psychiatrists . . . You know, they were trying to get Ruby off scot-free, and make him out a hero.

In his closing argument to the jury, Belli said: "You cannot find this sick man guilty of anything. It would be an incongruity to compromise and say one year, two years, five years. . . . You can't arrogate unto yourselves, you good jurors in this good town, the right to put a sick man in jail for six months, or to put a stigma on him by a suspended sentence" (Statement of Facts, 124, 125).

JMD: Do you remember anything specifically about Dr. Gibbs, the last witness to testify in the trial. He made a dramatic appearance at the very end.

RF: No, I really don't.

JMD: If you had been doing the defense for Ruby, how might you have done it differently?

RF: Oh, I think probably I would have thrown myself on the mercy of the court, in light of the fact that they had television tape [and] they showed it to us, of Ruby shooting him [Oswald]. If they would have said he got caught up in the moment and was sorry for John Kennedy, little John, and his [JFK's] wife, and he [Ruby] did wrong, I think probably it would have been better. That's what I would have done. I don't know if it would have been any different, but I just think that would have been better. Rather than say, well, for an hour or so the man had this lapse of right and wrong and just killed him. But they were saying, well, he did this and so what he needs to do is go to a shrink for a few months, and put him back out in society. . . . If you read the transcript, and you look at it, you see that we didn't have much choice. It was either let him go to the shrink for a little bit, and turn him loose, or give him the death penalty.

JMD: Do you have memories of the jury deliberations?

RF: No, not really.

JMD: Do you recall how long it took?

RF: Gosh, I don't know. Seems like it took us two or three hours. I don't remember, honestly.

JMD: Max [Causey] wrote in his diary that he initially argued against the death penalty, mainly so that somebody would make that argument. He didn't want it to be an open-and-shut kind of thing.

RF: I remember it took us a little time, because each one had something to say. And I remember Max went around the room and had everybody say what they said.

JMD: Why the death penalty? Did you, at that time, feel that was the only punishment for such a major crime?

RF: Well, as I remember the charge they gave us, we could either find him insane for a little bit, and let him go to a psychiatrist and have some treatment, or we could turn him loose. It was either/or, you know. So I just don't think any of us [felt] like that we could say, well, he went nuts for ten minutes and then he was OK. I mean, I think it was pretty much premeditated.

Judge Brown's charge to the jury said in part: "If the defendant was not of sound mind but was affected with insanity and such affection, if any, was the cause of the alleged act . . . then he ought to be acquitted" (Kaplan and Waltz 1965, 308–309).

With respect to giving Ruby the death penalty, Causey wrote that several jurors placed great importance on having said during their qualifying examinations that they would vote for death if it was proven to them that Ruby was guilty and acted with malice in killing Oswald.

JMD: You said [before the interview] you did receive some threatening phone calls.

RF: Well, I had a few phone calls and I had quite a few letters telling me that I was going to hell and all this kind of stuff. And there were people waiting on me when I'd get home at night. So, I had to find a place to stay for two or three weeks where I could just take my family. You know, everybody wanted to talk to me. It was . . .

JMD: Not a pleasant situation?

RF: No.

JMD: And that went on for several weeks?

RF: I'd say two or three weeks, yeah. So I just moved out. And we stayed gone for a couple of weeks, and the neighbors told us that people stopped coming over there, so it kind of died down a little bit.

JMD: And you also received letters?

RF: Uh, huh [yes].

JMD: Did you turn these over to the police or did you ever talk to the police about it?

RF: Oh, I think I called Bo [Mabra, the bailiff] about 'em, or somebody, just to let 'em know. But I threw 'em away.

JMD: What was the basis of their anger?

RF: I think mainly that we gave him the death penalty.

JMD: These were people who felt that he was some sort of hero for killing Oswald?

RF: Yeah. I wish I could remember more about them. I probably should have kept them. I just threw everything away. I mean there were magazines that had our pictures in them, and all that, and that's all thrown away. And people ask me, why didn't you keep that stuff? I don't know. But there was a *Life* magazine, there was a French magazine [*Paris Match*].

JMD: *Newsweek*?

RF: Yeah, several pictures in there. And I think there's a picture of the jury downtown at that John F. Kennedy memorial [the Sixth Floor Museum].

JMD: Do you ever give the trial much thought, in the years since, or have you just completely left it behind?

RF: No, I haven't given it much thought. But the only thing that I thought was, you know, he [Ruby] died in jail of whatever [cancer-related causes], and so he wasn't electrocuted. So, we didn't, in essence, we didn't really . . . you know, although we found him guilty, he never was electrocuted.

JMD: In some ways, was that a relief?

RF: Yeah, I'd be lying if I didn't say it was. I hated that he died of cancer, but it's just kind of like something else took care of it, I don't know.

JMD: Never any second thoughts, or did you ever say, boy, I wish we'd done something differently? Or any piece of information that might have come up that might have made you wish you'd known that at the time?

RF: No, no.

JMD: I read that the Texas Court of Criminal Appeals overturned the decision in '66 because the trial was kept in Dallas. At the time that happened, did that make you angry?

RF: No, I don't remember any of that.

JMD: It was not your problem at that point, you didn't have to worry about it anymore?

RF: Yeah, that's right.

JMD: And then he [Ruby] died in early '67 before they could retry him.

RF: I was so busy trying to make a living for my family . . .

JMD: You told me [before the interview] that this actually hurt your career, missing all that time at work.

RF: Well, it was just the fact that when I got back, they were not going to pay for the time I was off, which I thought was against the law. But they did, they did pay me. But because of that, we never got along too well after that. I left . . . I wasn't there very long.

JMD: Got off on a bad foot?

RF: Yeah. And it wasn't my fault. But, it was just one of those things that happened. I don't know why they weren't going to pay me, but, I guess, you know, you hire somebody and the first day they're supposed to come to work they've got to report for jury duty. I think it was the second or third day [on the job] I went down there, and I was picked, and then I was gone for seventeen days. So basically, I was gone a month. And I come back and they're not going to pay me, and I've got a family, and, you know, I was living hand-to-mouth. . . . I think being on the jury, they were paying us $5 a day or something, I can't remember how much it was. [A *Dallas Morning News* article at the time of the trial reported the jurors were paid $8 per day.] But that's what happened.

JMD: You did what you were asked to do, did your duty.

RF: That's what I did, yeah, tried to do what I thought was right.

J. G. (Glenn) Holton, Jr.

J. G. (Glenn) Holton, Jr., was the eighth juror chosen for the Jack Ruby trial. A career U.S. Postal Service employee, at the time of this interview he was still working as a postal carrier.

JMD: Max [Causey] once said that when he got the notice for jury duty, he quickly had the sense it was for the Ruby trial.

GH: Yeah, me too. Yeah, I told my boss when I left that day, "I won't see you for two or three months." I had that feeling.

JMD: I read that you were on a fishing trip and did not see the killing of Oswald on TV.

GH: Yeah, I was doing something, I don't remember what it was.

JMD: Did you ever see a replay before the trial began, or had you not seen it at all?

GH: I might have seen it on the television days and weeks later.

JMD: You don't have any specific memory of having seen it?

GH: No.

JMD: Melvin Belli wrote extensively about the jury selection process, and about each juror, and a little bit about why each juror was selected. His impression was that you were "emotional" about the case. Do you remember it that way?

GH: No, I wasn't emotional.

JMD: You didn't have strong personal feelings about the case?

GH: Uh, uh [no].

JMD: You were on the police reserve in Grand Prairie?

GH: Yeah, in the mid-'60s, I was a reserve on the Grand Prairie police force.

Holton's status as a reserve police officer was of some concern to the defense (Belli 1964, 137–38), but he testified that he had not been called up to serve in any capacity during the weekend of the assassination of Oswald's killing (Statement of Facts, 1689).

JMD: Why do you think you were chosen for the jury?

GH: Probably because I was an honest person, I imagine.

JMD: Did you have the sense they were looking for any particular personality traits?

GH: No, I didn't have any idea what they were doing. I never gave it any thought.

Belli (1964, 137–138) wrote: "Juror eight . . . was a fleshy-faced, deeply tanned mail carrier in a gray checked sport jacket. His name was J. G. Holton, Jr., and he lived in suburban Grand Prairie. He was also a member of the Grand Prairie police reserve. . . . He said he had spent the entire tragic weekend away on a fishing trip. I wrote, 'Emotional. He's police reserve. He was away fishing. Seemed to appreciate that many people emotional—would have shot Oswald. Didn't move hands [Belli believed this was very important in determining someone's sincerity]. Believes cap punishment.'"

JMD: What were your feelings about being chosen? Were you excited about it, or were you apprehensive about it, wish it hadn't happened?

GH: No, not really. I liked it. I really enjoyed it.

JMD: Did you enjoy the time you spent? Once you got into it, you enjoyed the experience?

GH: Sure did. Didn't bother me at all.

One of the jurors, Mrs. Mildred McCollum, was quoted after the trial as saying the jurors were "an extremely compatible group." She said the jurors pooled their resources during the trial to make their quarters more pleasant. One juror [Allen McCoy], she said, contributed a stereo and others had records brought in. They were allowed to watch television except for the news, and some stayed up as late as 2 A.M. watching late-night movies ("Jury Compatible," 1964).

In another article, Mrs. McCollum said, "I did accomplish one thing during the three weeks we were locked up. I managed to figure my income taxes" (Millsap 1964, 16-A).

JMD: Did you ever get any threatening letters or calls?

GH: No, they told me they intercepted all those, and I think they threw 'em all away.

JMD: Who did? Your family?

GH: I think the bailiff of the court did. Yeah, everything I got was from little kids.

JMD: The Causeys got some, I would not call them threatening letters, but they were hateful.

GH: Is that right?

JMD: Months or years after the trial, did anybody ever send you anything that you considered threatening?

GH: Never did, never got anything.

JMD: That's good, because the potential was there for that kind of reaction.

GH: Oh, yeah.

JMD: There's always been the discussion about whether the trial should have been moved from Dallas. What was your opinion about that at the time and has your opinion changed at all over the years?

GH: My opinion is no matter where they had the trial the results would probably be the same.

JMD: So even if they had moved it to Houston . . .

GH: Wouldn't have made a difference.

JMD: Why do you think that's so?

GH: Well, you know, if a person is guilty, they're guilty.

JMD: Belli complained that the jury members were too much alike, that they were all basically middle-class, white, Protestant people, no Jews, and, of course, Ruby was Jewish. As you look back on it, do you feel that played any role in the outcome of the trial?

GH: No, it didn't have. . . . I think there were about four women on the trial [jury] and they all felt, kind of, just the opposite as the men did. But when we got through hashing it out, we all decided to give him death.

JMD: When you say they felt opposite as the men did, you mean they were initially opposed to the death penalty?

GH: Mm-hmm [yes].

JMD: But they agreed with everyone else on guilt or innocence?

GH: Oh, yeah.

JMD: It's amazing the amount of press coverage of this trial, all over the world, even to the point of stories about each juror. Were you struck by that? Of course, you may not have realized it at the time.

GH: No, I didn't realize it till later on, till they gave me some of these magazines, like this French magazine [*Paris Match*].

JMD: Were you surprised by that?

GH: Not really.

JMD: It was a major event.

GH: It sure was.

Scrutiny of the jury was such that public television commentator Jim Lehrer, then a reporter for the *Dallas Times Herald*, wrote an article analyzing the manner in which the jury filed into court each day. Lehrer noted that the jurors walked into the courtroom in the same order each day and "matter-of-factly went to their chairs like school children in a seat-charted classroom." Lehrer noted that a "pet theory" held that the first juror into the courtroom each day would likely be the foreman. This proved incorrect, as Allen McCoy regularly led the others in. Some observers believed that the fact that the jurors were so methodical meant they were a "hanging jury"; others held that such a jury would likely be one that returns an acquittal verdict.

Lehrer commented that all of the jurors wore "no-nonsense" expressions on their faces. Occasionally something funny would happen in the courtroom and everyone would laugh, Lehrer wrote. "Everybody, that is, except eight men and four women in the jury box. As far as anybody has seen, not as much as a grin has come yet on any of the 12 faces" (Lehrer, "Ruby Jury," 1964).

JMD: You said [before the interview] that people asked you about it for several years after the trial.
GH: Several years afterwards, and then people forgot about it.
JMD: When people asked you about it, what did they want to know?
GH: Oh, a lot of 'em asked me about ol' Belli [chuckles].
JMD: I want to ask you your impressions of several of the people involved in the trial. What were your impressions of Belli?
GH: Oh, I thought he was a real good lawyer and everything, colorful, and, you know, he just stood out like a star. But, you know, he was fighting a pretty tough battle.
JMD: He had a lot of negative things to say about Dallas, and, after the trial, he was critical of the jury for the verdict. You took no offense at that?
GH: No, no. I didn't pay a lot of attention afterwards, [and] I didn't pay a lot of attention before it all happened. You know, back then, I was doing a lot of fishing. I was a commercial fisherman, plus I worked at the post office. So I just went back to doing what I was doing. Within a few months, hardly anyone said anything about it [chuckles].

A few minutes after the verdict was announced, Belli, speaking with reporters, said Ruby had been "railroaded," that the trial had been conducted in a "kangaroo court," and that the jurors had made Dallas "a city of shame forever more" (Belli 1964, 257).

JMD: What were your impressions of Ruby? He must have sat there quietly during the trial, but did you form any impressions of him?
GH: No, not really. Most of the time, I was just mainly listening to ol' Belli and then the district attorney. They were, kind of, the two stars, you might say.
JMD: Henry Wade was quite a character too, wasn't he?
GH: Oh, yeah, he was.

JMD: What were your memories of him?

GH: Oh, he kind of reminded me of a Baptist preacher, when he gets up there and starts ranting and raving and everything. Like I said, all my impressions of everybody were good.

JMD: How about the judge, Joe Brown?

GH: Yeah, he was a good ol' guy. Yeah, there was one time I was sick and we had a little scheme there, that if I had to run I'd raise my hand and wave it at him, and he'd just dismiss the jury, and we'd all go [laughs].

JMD: Belli had some criticisms of Judge Brown, saying that he ruled too often in favor of the prosecution, and that had an impact on the outcome of the trial. Is that in line with your memory of how things went?

GH: Well, I thought he was fair to both sides. Never entered my mind [that he favored the prosecution].

JMD: He was a very easy-going kind of guy.

GH: Yeah, easy-going person. He kind of let everybody do their thing, and do it in order.

JMD: Do you have any memories of Max [Causey], as the foreman?

GH: Very little. I got those pictures out again, and was looking at them, and there's a few people I remember. Yeah, I remember this one lady. She was white-haired, and she said the reason she was white-haired, her son nearly choked to death one night, and a few days later, her hair turned completely white.

The selection of Mrs. Louise Malone, the juror to whom Holton was referring, was sardonically described by Melvin Belli, who regarded her with suspicion because of her relation to a prominent Dallas police officer (1964, p. 143): "Juror number twelve was the aunt of the Dallas Police Department's public relations officer. Her name was Mrs. Louis [sic] Malone. His name was Art Hammett, and he was a personable young man who could be seen regularly on television in a show extolling various aspects of the fine work the department was doing." Defense attorney Joe Tonahill asked for an additional peremptory challenge to excuse Mrs. Malone, but he was turned down by Judge Frank Wilson, who was substituting that day for Judge Brown.

JMD: And there's never been anytime when the jurors got back together again?

GH: No one's ever even called me in all these thirty-four or thirty-five years.

JMD: Was being sequestered unpleasant for you?

GH: No, no. There was, I can't remember everybody's name now, but there was one guy, he was a business salesman, and, boy, he wanted to get things going. He wanted to get in and get out. He was losing money. Of course, I worked for the post office. I didn't have to worry about it. I was on "cold leave," what they call it.

JMD: Where were you sequestered?

GH: They put us up on the top of one of those courthouses. I think it was the one right across the street from the new one now. They had a bunch of little rooms up there, they were all about 8-by-10 [feet], something like that. Everyone had this little room.

JMD: Not luxurious quarters.

GH: No, it was adequate.

JMD: When you think back about the trial itself, Belli and the defense presented an insanity defense and presented a lot of evidence that Ruby was unstable. What was your thought process in assessing the evidence that they presented?

GH: Well, that [psycho]motor epilepsy stuff didn't make much sense. It was weak. I didn't latch on to a lot of it. I just thought he [Belli] was trying to get him off on an insane plea, or something like that. I just kind of figured ol' Ruby just went off his rocker and got mad and wanted to shoot somebody. That was a good way of getting even [for the assassination of President Kennedy].

JMD: Just getting mad doesn't constitute insanity?

GH: No, it sure don't. Just like people get drunk and kill people, I don't believe that's an excuse either, because they were sober before they got drunk. I think anybody who goes into a rage could do about anything to somebody. But they don't get off on insanity pleas. They [the defense] just presented an individual that on the spur of the moment pulled out a gun and shot someone, went "temporarily insane," probably for about two seconds [chuckles], you might say.

JMD: So it's another way of saying you think he lost his temper, he just got angry.

GH: Yeah, anybody can get angry, but you have to suffer your consequences.

JMD: Then getting angry, extremely angry, is not the same as being temporarily insane?

GH: No, I don't think so. Anybody can throw a fit.

JMD: Did you have the sense there was any significant premeditation of the shooting or do you think this was something he did more or less on the spur of the moment?

GH: He probably did it on the spur of the moment. He was around the police all the time, doing this and doing that.

Both sides attempted to use Ruby's apparently normal demeanor just before and during the shooting as evidence of his sanity or insanity. Belli tried to use the testimony of Dallas police officer James Leavelle to help make his case that Ruby was temporarily insane. Under questioning by Belli, Leavelle testified he had known Ruby casually for eight to ten years, and did not consider him "peculiar." Belli, attempting to show that Ruby did not know what he was doing, asked Leavelle if Ruby's face was "agitated" as he charged Oswald. Leavelle said no. During redirect examination, Assistant District Attorney Bill Alexander asked Leavelle if he was looking at Ruby's face or the gun as Ruby stepped toward Oswald. "My attention was fastened more on the pistol [a Colt Cobra .38]," Leavelle said.

During the testimony of Western Union supervisor Doyle Lane, who sold Ruby a money order to send to one of his dancers four minutes before the shooting, District Attorney Henry Wade asked if Ruby was "excitedly fumbling with any money or in a state of agitation." Lane said no. He appeared to be "cool, calm and outwardly collected?" Wade asked. Lane replied, "That is correct." Lane went on to say Ruby walked toward City Hall, where the jail was housed, about 300 feet away, at an "ordinary pace" (Statement of Facts, 143, 145, 197–198, 202).

JMD: With respect to the psychiatrists who testified on behalf of Jack Ruby, in general, why were they not more convincing to you?

GH: Well, I think the way most of us felt, we really didn't feel too much about psychiatrists in the first place. I think nowadays [people] think a little bit more about them.

JMD: So it was a general lack of acceptance of what psychiatrists might bring to the case.

GH: Yeah, I think nowadays if they had the trial, people would think a little bit different, maybe, but then, we just . . . that's the way I felt.

JMD: Did you feel as if they were perhaps trying to—not the psychiatrists themselves, but the defense by presenting the psychiatrists—put something over on you?

GH: Yeah, that's the way I kind of felt about it.

JMD: What was your thinking in deciding [to give] the death penalty?

GH: I'm just a believer that if you take someone's life, your life needs to be taken. That's the way I've always felt. Unfortunately, there were three or four people on the jury that didn't feel that way. But we finally talked them into agreeing with the other eight.

JMD: What were the deliberations like?

GH: Well, it's hard to remember. I know your uncle [Max Causey] did most of the talking. And a few other people said a few things. And then some of them wanted to, I think, give him life, or something or other like that. But, like I said, we didn't do much arguing. Some people just said what they thought, and by the time everyone said their feelings, we just [voted] to give him that capital verdict and execute him.

JMD: Do you remember how long you were out?

GH: It wasn't very long. It sure wasn't. In fact, I think we got out about noon. I think we might have only been down there about two or three hours.

JMD: Max writes in his diary that he initially argued against the death penalty even though he was sort of in favor of it himself, because he thought there should be some kind of debate. Do you remember that?

GH: No, not really. Like I say, I remember there were three or four. They didn't really want the death penalty, but by the time we got through having a little discussion, everyone agreed.

JMD: There was no sense of the death penalty being necessary to wipe the slate clean for Dallas?

GH: No, like I say, I just have my beliefs—that if you kill somebody, the state needs to take [your life].

JMD: Do you have any thoughts about how, if you were conducting the defense, you might have presented it differently, and what might have been more effective?

GH: Yeah, well, that happened so long ago. But, I would have kind of thrown a little more mercy on the jury, to be kind, you know what I mean? Now, it seems like to me that [Belli] didn't exactly do it that way. He had all this theory about this psychiatrists' stuff and so forth, and hardly anybody swallowed it, too much. It seemed like to me that he didn't put it on the mercy of the jury.

JMD: Two years later, the Court of Criminal Appeals overturned the trial and ordered a new trial, I think mainly because [the court] said the trial should have been moved out of Dallas.

GH: Is that right?

JMD: You don't remember that?

GH: I don't remember all that.

JMD: You don't have a memory of how you felt about all that?

GH: Sure don't.

JMD: I get the impression this has not been a central event in your life at all, just one brief episode that you more or less just put out of your mind once it was over. Is that correct?

GH: Yeah, I've always looked forward. I try and never look back.

JMD: In the intervening years, have you ever thought about it, had any kind of reflection on it, and said, "Well, we might have done this or that differently?"

GH: No, I wouldn't change anything or do anything different whatsoever. I think justice was served.

JMD: You know, people won't let it go, and I guess I'm an example of that. . . . People keep trying to tie Ruby in with the assassination of Kennedy in some way, keep trying to link Ruby and Oswald, Ruby was trying to silence Oswald. Do you give any credence to any of those conspiracy theories?

GH: All that stuff? No, every time someone gets shot, they have a bunch of different theories about this and that. But, it's just [that] the people just don't want to let something die.

JMD: From what you knew about Ruby and what was presented in the trial, do you think he was capable of being involved in something of that order?

GH: Well, I found out later on he was nothing but a hoodlum, but I didn't know what he was when we were in the trial. Yeah, I've heard about the Mafia ties, well, same way with Frank Sinatra. They tried to connect him to the Mafia, too.

JMD: So, none of that was presented during the trial, his background?

GH: I don't think it was, you know, I don't remember anything like that.

JMD: Have you ever served on any juries since that time?

GH: No, I've been over there plenty of times, but I don't get put on nothing anymore [chuckles]. Absolutely nothing. I couldn't even get on an apartment jury one time.

JMD: On a what?

GH: Well, they had a little jury over in Garland. They were kicking these people out of their apartment, for breaking some rules, and I couldn't even get on that one.

JMD: Do you still fish?

GH: I haven't wet a hook in two years. In fact, what messed myself up, I sold my old Buick that had a bumper hitch on it, and I haven't got around to putting a bumper hitch on any of my cars. Otherwise, I'd be fishing.

References

Aynesworth, Hugh. 21 February 1964. "Wife Says Mate to Be Good Juror." *Dallas Morning News* (page unknown). From collection of Max and Rosemary Causey.

Bedford, Sybille. 27 March 1964. "Violence, Froth, Sob Stuff—Was Justice Done?" *Life* 56, 13: 32–34, 70–74.

Belli, Melvin M. 1964. *Dallas Justice: The Real Story of Jack Ruby and His Trial.* New York: David McKay Company, Inc.

Biffle, Kent. 15 March 1964. "Juror Tries for Shut-Eye, but Without Much Success." *Dallas Morning News*, 16-A.

Causey, Keith. Interview by J. M. Dempsey, 5 March 2000.

Causey, Rosemary. Interview by J. M. Dempsey, 5 March 2000.

Conde, Carlos. 15 March 1964. "Most Agree Verdict Just; Some Persons Feel Penalty Too Severe." *Dallas Morning News*, 23-A.

"Cordiality Prevails at Trial." 5 March 1964. *Dallas Times Herald*, 6-A.

"Death for Ruby." 20 March 1964. *Time* 83: 27–8.

"Defense Employs Last Challenge." 2 March 1964. *Dallas Times Herald*, 1-A.

"Dwindling Ruby Juror Prospects to be Reinforced." 27 February 1964. *Dallas Times Herald*, 1-A.

Fenley, Bob. 1 March 1964. "First Testimony Nears for Ruby." *Dallas Times Herald*, 1-A.

Flechtner, Robert J. (Bob). Interview by J. M. Dempsey, 1998, 1999.

"Frightened by jailbreak." 7 March 1964. *Dallas Times Herald*, 10-A.

Holton, J. G. (Glenn), Jr. Interview by J. M. Dempsey, 1998, 1999.

"Juror Praised By Supervisor." 21 February 1964. *Dallas Times Herald* (page unknown). From collection of Max and Rosemary Causey.

"Jury 'Compatible' Group, Woman Says." 15 March 1964. *Greenville (Texas) Herald-Banner*, 1-A. From collection of Max and Rosemary Causey.

Kaplan, John and Jon R. Waltz. 1965. *The Trial of Jack Ruby*. New York: The Macmillan Company.

Kilgallen, Dorothy. 20 February 1964. "Ruby Trial: Dallas Irony." *Dallas Times Herald*, 1-A.

Lehrer, Jim. 21 February 1964. "Juror Faces Lonely Life Until Joined by Another." *Dallas Times Herald* (page unknown). From collection of Max and Rosemary Causey.

————. 5 March 1964. "Ruby Jury Always Seated Same Way." *Dallas Times Herald*, 6-A.

Lehrer, Jim and Jim Featherston. 7 March 1964. "Detectives Seize 5th Jail Escapee; 2 More Still Free in Daring Break." *Dallas Times Herald*, 1-A.

"Lone Ruby Juror Gets 8-Foot Square Room." 21 February 1964. *Dallas Morning News* (page unknown). From collection of Max and Rosemary Causey.

Martin, Dan. 15 March 1964. "Jurors Away or Mum." *Dallas Morning News*, 16-A.

Mathias, Paul. 7 March 1964. "Maman Est En Prison: Elle Juge Ruby." *Paris Match* 778: 98–101. Translated by Suzanne (Maples) Dougherty, Commerce, Texas, 1965.

Millsap, Don. 15 March 1964. "Juror 'Glad to be Home.'" *Dallas Morning News*, 16-A.

"Nobody is hardly ever mad enough to be a mad man." July 1963. *Science Digest* 54: 57–8.

"Objection sustained; to get new trial." 17 October 1966. *Time* 68: 31.

"Redefining insanity." 29 November 1963. *Time* 82: 54.

Richmond, Jerry and Bob Fenley. 4 March 1964. "First Witnesses Call Ruby Volatile As Prosecution Starts Building Case." *Dallas Times Herald*, 1-A.

Rose, J. Waymon. Interview by J. M. Dempsey, March 2000.

Rothwell, Gina (Causey). Interview by J. M. Dempsey, 5 March 2000.

Rubenstein, J., alias Jack Ruby, appellant v. The State of Texas, appellee, No. 37900, 407 S.W. 2d 793, Court of Criminal Appeals of Texas, 5 October 1966.

Schmalleger, Frank. 1999. "Schmalleger's Glossary." Available at http://
    /talkjustice.com/files/glossary.htm. Accessed July 1999.

"7th Juror Selected for Trial of Jack Ruby." 26 February 1964. *Dallas
    Times Herald*, 1-A.

"Shame of Dallas, Texas." 11 April 1964. *Saturday Evening Post* 237:
    82.

"Shouter, Shooter, No Juror." 21 February 1964. *Dallas Times Herald*,
    3-A.

Sowell, Douglas J. Interview by J. M. Dempsey, 1998, 1999.

Statement of Facts. The State of Texas vs. Jack Rubenstein alias Jack
    Ruby. Criminal District Court No. 3, Dallas, Texas. No. E-4010-J.

Watson, Constance. February 1964. "Family Misses Juror." *Dallas
    Times Herald* (page and date unknown). From the collection of
    Max and Rosemary Causey.

Weinberg, Stan and Jerry Richmond. 19 February 1964. "All On Jury
    Panel Who Saw Slaying Facing Subpoenas." *Dallas Times Herald*, 1-A.

Index

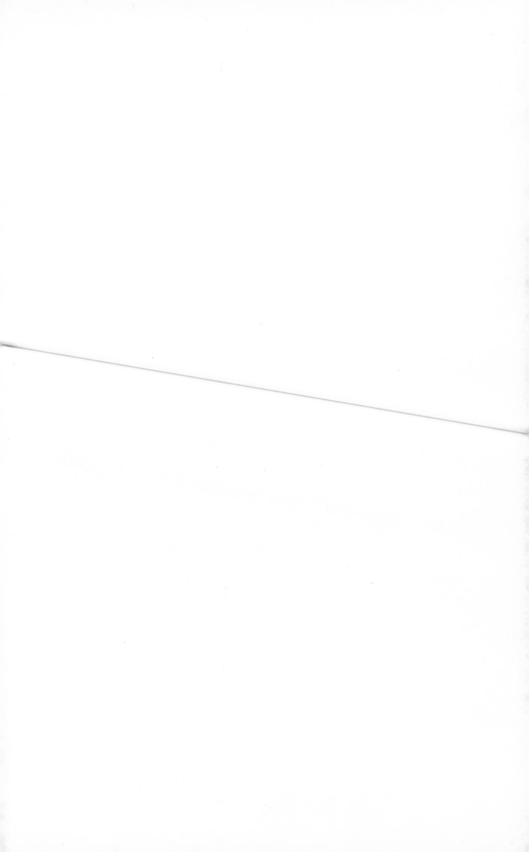